OXFORD ST
Series Edit

CW01501172

19th & 20th Century Women Poets

✳

Edited by
Elizabeth Gurr and Celia de Piro

Oxford University Press

Oxford University Press, Great Clarendon Street, Oxford OX2 6DP

Oxford New York
Athens Auckland Bangkok Bogota Bombay
Buenos Aires Calcutta Cape Town Dar es Salaam Delhi
Florence Hong Kong Istanbul Karachi
Kuala Lumpur Madras Madrid Melbourne
Mexico City Nairobi Paris Singapore
Taipei Tokyo Toronto

and associated companies in
Berlin Ibadan

Oxford is a trade mark of Oxford University Press

First published by Oxford University Press
ISBN 0 19 831990 8

Other titles in the series

Blake: Songs of Innocence and of Experience	0 19 831952 5
Chaucer: General Prologue to the Canterbury Tales	0 19 831967 3
Chaucer: The Miller's Tale	0 19 831988 6
Chaucer: The Nun's Priest's Tale	0 19 831987 8
John Donne: Selected Poems	0 19 831950 9
Christopher Fry: The Lady's Not For Burning	0 19 831959 2
Thomas Hardy: Selected Poems	0 19 831963 0
Gerard Manley Hopkins: Selected Poems	0 19 831961 4
D.H. Lawrence: Selected Poems	0 19 831962 2
Alexander Pope: The Rape of the Lock	0 19 831958 4
Six Women Poets	0 19 833181 9
William Wordsworth: Selected Poems	0 19 881951 7
W.B. Yeats: Selected Poems	0 19 831966 5

Typeset by AFS Image Setters Ltd, Glasgow

Printed in the United Kingdom at the University Press, Cambridge

The cover illustration is by John Rushton.

Contents

Acknowledgements

We are grateful for permission to reproduce copyright poems:

Eavan Boland: all poems reprinted from *Collected Poems* by Eavan Boland (Carcanet, 1995) by permission of Carcanet Press Ltd.

Emily Dickinson: all poems reprinted from *The Poems of Emily Dickinson*, [3 volumes] edited by Thomas H. Johnson, Cambridge, Mass.: The Belknap Press of Harvard University Press, Copyright © 1951, 1955, 1979, 1983 by the President and Fellows of Harvard College; by permission of the publishers and the Trustees of Amherst College; poems 251 [p.24], 341 [p.27], and 419 [p.28] also reprinted from *The Complete Poems of Emily Dickinson*, edited by Thomas H. Johnson, Copyright © 1929, 1935 by Martha Dickinson Bianchi; Copyright © renewed 1957, 1963 by Mary L. Hampson, by permission of the publishers, Little, Brown & Company.

Carol Ann Duffy: 'Head of English', 'Ash Wednesday 1984', 'Words of Absolution', 'Standing Female Nude', 'A Healthy Meal', 'Letters from Deadmen' and 'The Dolphins' are taken from *Standing Female Nude* by Carol Ann Duffy published by Anvil Press Poetry in 1985; 'Recognition', 'Psychopath', 'The Virgin Punishing the Infant' and 'Foreign' are taken from *Selling Manhattan* by Carol Ann Duffy published by Anvil Press Poetry in 1987; 'Making Money' is taken from *The Other Country* by Carol Ann Duffy published by Anvil Press Poetry in 1990; 'The Grammar of Light', 'Prayer' and 'Small Female Skull' are taken from *Mean Time* by Carol Ann Duffy published by Anvil Press Poetry in 1993; all poems reprinted by permission of Anvil Press Poetry Ltd.

Elizabeth Jennings: all poems reprinted from *Collected Poems* by Elizabeth Jennings (Macmillan) by permission of David Higham Associates on behalf of the author.

Sylvia Plath: all poems reprinted from *Collected Poems* by Sylvia Plath (Faber, 1981) by permission of Faber & Faber Ltd.

We are also grateful to the following poets for providing introductions to their poems:

Eavan Boland: Introduction © Eavan Boland, 1997.
Carol Ann Duffy: Introduction © Carol Ann Duffy, 1997.
Elizabeth Jennings: Introduction © Elizabeth Jennings, 1997.

The poets in this selection appear in chronological order with the exception of Jennings and Plath. Due to Plath's early death, this reversal seemed appropriate to a study of the development of women's poetry across two centuries.

Editors

Dr Victor Lee
Dr Victor Lee, the Series Editor, read English at University College, Cardiff. He was awarded a doctorate at Oxford University. He has experience of teaching at Secondary and Tertiary level, and is currently working at the Open University. Victor Lee has been Chief Examiner in English for three examination boards over a period of twenty-five years.

Elizabeth Gurr
Elizabeth Gurr was born in New Zealand and educated there and at Oxford. She has taught in schools, colleges and universities in England and Africa and was Head of English at the Holt school in Berkshire for seventeen years. She is married with three sons and the author of *Alexander Pope* in the Writer and Critics series (Oliver and Boyd) and editor of *Pope: The Rape of the Lock* in the Oxford Student Texts series.

Celia de Piro
Celia de Piro was born and educated in Yorkshire. After reading English she was awarded the Wordsworth Research Fellowship at St Hugh's College, Oxford where she spent some years in research and teaching. She has since been a Senior Lecturer in a College of Education, a tutor for the Open University, and an A-level examiner. She is currently teaching English at Cheltenham Ladies' College.

Foreword

Oxford Student Texts are specifically aimed at presenting poetry and drama to an audience which is studying English Literature at an advanced level. Each text is designed as an integrated whole consisting of three main parts. The poetry or the play is placed first to stress its importance and to encourage students to enjoy it without secondary critical material of any kind. When help is need on other occasions, the second and third parts of these texts, the Notes and the Approaches provide it.

The Notes perform two functions. First, they provide information and explain allusions. Secondly, and this is where they differ from most texts at this level, they often raise questions of central concern to the interpretation of the poem or the play being dealt with, particularly in the use of a general note placed at the beginning of the particular notes.

The third part, the Approaches section, deals with major issues of response to the particular section of poetry or drama, as opposed to the work of the writer as a whole. One of the major aims of this part of the text is to emphasize that there is no one right answer to interpretation, but a series of approaches. Readers are given guidance as to what counts as evidence, but, in the end, left to make up their mind as to which are the most suitable interpretations, or to add their own.

To help achieve this, the Approaches section contains a number of activity-discussion sequences, although it must be stressed that these are optional. Significant issues about the poem or the play are raised in these activities. Readers are invited to tackle these activities before proceeding to the discussion section where possible responses to the questions raised in the activities are considered. Their main function is to engage readers actively in the ideas of the text. However, these activity-discussion sequences are so arranged that, if readers wish to treat the Approaches as continuous prose and not attempt the activities, they can.

At the end of each text there is also a list of Tasks. Whereas the activity-discussion sequences are aimed at increasing understanding of the literary work itself, these tasks are intended to help explore ideas about the poetry or the play after the student has completed the reading of the work and the studying of the Notes and Approaches. These tasks are particularly helpful for coursework projects or in preparing for an examination.

Victor Lee   *Series Editor*

The Poems

Introduction to Emily Brontë

In 1848, Charlotte Brontë wrote of her sister's poetry:

> I know – no woman that ever lived – ever wrote such poetry before –
> Condensed energy, clearness, finish, strange, strong, pathos are
> their characteristics – utterly different from the weak diffusiveness –
> the laboured yet most feeble wordiness [of] which dilute the writings
> of even very popular poetesses. (Juliet Barker, *The Brontës*, p.484)

Brontë was born in July 1818, the fifth of six children. Her father, the Reverend Patrick Brontë, was curate of Haworth, a small mill town high on the Yorkshire moors. He was an indomitable figure: a widower who, on his death in 1861, had seen all his children go to early graves. At the age of six Brontë was sent to a charity school for the daughters of impoverished clergy at Cowan Bridge. This became the model for Lowood Institute, the notorious school in Charlotte Brontë's *Jane Eyre*. Emily hated the cold morality of the strict Calvinist regime and she was to oppose it fiercely all her life. She was withdrawn from school, along with her three sisters after six months when an infectious fever (probably tubercular) broke out. Maria and Elizabeth aged 10 and 11 died soon afterwards and so began the family history of failing health and early death.

Winters at Haworth parsonage were lonely and snow-bound, images of which appear repeatedly in Emily's poetry, but the Brontë children were precocious and self-sufficient, entertaining themselves by writing stories and plays. These grew into the chronicles of Angria and Gondal which they wrote in minuscule handwriting in tiny books. Anne and Emily wrote about Gondal, an island in the north Pacific. The stories were pure Gothic fantasy - deeds of chivalry, political intrigue, romantic lore and heroic battle. Emily's contributions, highly coloured by her love of Scott, Milton and a writer of graveside ballads in *Blackwood's Magazine*, reveal an early morbid preoccupation with death.

1

As an adolescent she grew steadily more reclusive. There is no record of her having made a single friend outside the family. This self-imposed isolation may explain that intensity of suppressed feeling which characterizes her work. Unlike her sisters, she had no interest whatsoever in the opposite sex. Her writing was all consuming; she out-manoeuvred Anne and Charlotte and remained at home as her father's housekeeper rather than take up a post as a governess. Her brief period in Brussels in 1842 as a music teacher was a misery. Taunts about her unbecoming dress received the reply, *I wish to be as God made me.* Professor Héger (the husband of the Principal of the school where Charlotte and Emily were pupil-teachers) later stated that he considered her genius superior to Charlotte's but found her unsociable, believing she exerted *a kind of unconscious tyranny* over her sister. (Juliet Barker, *The Brontës*, p.392.) Her essays at this time show an unsentimental but passionate love of animals, her doubt in divine retribution and a fascination with heroic death.

In 1844 she began to extract her poems from their prose context and copy them into two notebooks – the 'Gondal Notebook' (44 poems) and 'Untitled Notebook' (31 poems). Unfortunately she did not keep the distinction clear and continued the Gondal narrative up to her death. It is therefore difficult to be sure which, if any, poems are truly personal. Reluctantly she agreed to publish them on condition that the Gondal origins be disguised and her identity concealed under the pseudonym Ellis Bell. However, without the Gondal background, some seemed difficult to understand and the book was ignored, though one reviewer described her as a *fine quaint spirit*. No one but her sisters recognized the great originality of thought and expression, the fine feeling for nature and an unusual mystical quality. Failure possibly caused her to turn from poetry to prose. Her great and only novel *Wuthering Heights* appeared, again at her own cost, in December 1847.

At the funeral of her brother Branwell she caught cold and the deadly symptoms began. She refused medicine or a doctor, and died on December 19th 1848, aged 30 – a woman of unconquerable will, but also a troubled spirit yearning for an unattainable ideal.

'High waving heather 'neath stormy blasts bending'

High waving heather 'neath stormy blasts bending
Midnight and moonlight and bright shining stars
Darkness and glory rejoicingly blending
Earth rising to heaven and heaven descending
Man's spirit away from its drear dungeon sending
Bursting the fetters and breaking the bars

All down the mountain sides wild forests lending
One mighty voice to the life giving wind
Rivers their banks in the jubilee rending
10 Fast through the valleys a reckless course wending
Wider and deeper their waters extending
Leaving a desolate desert behind

Shining and lowering and swelling and dying
Changing forever from midnight to noon
Roaring like thunder like soft music sighing
Shadows on shadows advancing and flying
Lightning bright flashes the deep gloom defying
Coming as swiftly and fading as soon

'And first an hour of mournful musing'

And first an hour of mournful musing
And then a gush of bitter tears
And then a dreary calm diffusing
Its deadly mist o'er joys and cares

And then a throb and then a lightening
And then a breathing from above
And then a star in heaven brightening
The star the glorious star of love

'I'm happiest when most away'

I'm happiest when most away
I can bear my soul from its home of clay
On a windy night when the moon is bright
And my eye can wander through worlds of light

When I am not and none beside
Nor earth nor sea nor cloudless sky
But only spirit wandering wide
Through infinite immensity

To the Blue Bell

Sacred watcher, wave thy bells!
Fair hill flower and woodland child!
Dear to me in deep green dells—
Dearest on the mountains wild—

Blue bell, even as all divine
I have seen my darling shine—
Blue bell, even as wan and frail
I have seen my darling fail—
Thou hast found a voice for me—
10   And soothing words are breathed by thee—

Thus they murmur, 'Summer's sun
Warms me till my life is done—
Would I rather choose to die
Under winter's ruthless sky?

'Glad I bloom and calm I fade
Weeping twilight dews my bed
Mourner, mourner dry thy tears.
Sorrow comes with lengthened years!'

A Farewell to Alexandria

I've seen this dell in July's shine
As lovely as an angel's dream;
Above, heaven's depth of blue divine;
Around, the evening's golden beam—

I've seen the purple heather-bell
Look out by many a storm-worn stone
And oh, I've known such music swell,
Such wild notes wake these passes lone—

So soft, yet so intensely felt,
10 So low, yet so distinctly heard,
My breath would pause, my eyes would melt
And my tears dew the green heath-sward—

I'd linger here a summer day
Nor care how fast the hours flew by
Nor mark the sun's departing ray
Smile sadly glorious from the sky—

Then, then I might have laid thee down
And deemed thy sleep would gentle be
I might have left thee, darling one
20 And thought thy God was guarding thee!

But now, there is no wandering glow
No gleam to say that God is nigh:
And coldly spreads thy couch of snow
And harshly sounds thy lullaby.

Forests of heather dark and long
Wave their brown branching arms above
And they must soothe thee with their song
And they must shield my child of love!

Alas the flakes are heavily falling
30 They cover fast each guardian crest;
And chilly white their shroud is palling
Thy frozen limbs and freezing breast

Wakes up the storm more madly wild
The mountain drifts are tossed on high—
Farewell unblessed, unfriended child,
I cannot bear to watch thee die!

'And now the house dog stretched once more'

And now the house dog stretched once more
His limbs upon the glowing floor
The children half resumed their play
Though from the warm hearth scared away
The goodwife left her spinning wheel
And spread with smiles the evening meal
The Shepherd placed a seat and pressed
To their poor fare his unknown guest
And he unclasped his mantle now
10 And raised the covering from his brow
Said 'Voyagers by land and sea
Were seldom feasted daintily'
And checked his host by adding stern
He'd no refinement to unlearn
A silence settled on the room
The cheerful welcome sank to gloom

But not those words though cold and high
So froze their hospitable joy
No – there was something in his face
20 Some nameless thing they could not trace
And something in his voice's tone
Which turned their blood as chill as stone
The ringlets of his long black hair
Fell o'er a cheek most ghastly fair
Youthful he seemed – but worn as they
Who spend too soon their youthful day
When his glance drooped 'twas hard to quell
Unbidden feelings sudden swell
And pity scarce her tears could hide
30 So sweet that brow with all its pride
But when upraised his eye would dart
An icy shudder through the heart
Compassion changed to horror then
And fear to meet that gaze again
It was not hatred's tiger glare
Nor the wild anguish of despair
It was not useless misery
Which mocks at friendship's sympathy
No – lightning all unearthly shone
40 Deep in that dark eye's circling zone
Such withering lightning as we deem
None but a spectre's look may beam
And glad they were when he turned away
And wrapped him in his mantle grey
Leant down his head upon his arm
And veiled from view their basilisk charm

The Night-Wind

In summer's mellow midnight
A cloudless moon shone through
Our open parlour window
And rosetrees wet with dew

I sat in silent musing—
The soft wind waved my hair
It told me Heaven was glorious
And sleeping Earth was fair—

I needed not its breathing
10 To bring such thoughts to me
But still it whispered lowly
'How dark the woods will be!—

'The thick leaves in my murmur
Are rustling like a dream,
And all their myriad voices
Instinct with spirit seem'

I said, 'Go gentle singer,
Thy wooing voice is kind
But do not think its music
20 Has power to reach my mind—

'Play with the scented flower,
The young tree's supple bough—
And leave my human feelings
In their own course to flow'

The Wanderer would not leave me
Its kiss grew warmer still—
'O come,' it sighed so sweetly
'I'll win thee 'gainst thy will—

30 'Have we not been from childhood friends?
Have I not loved thee long?
As long as thou hast loved the night
Whose silence wakes my song?

'And when thy heart is laid at rest
Beneath the church-yard stone
I shall have time enough to mourn
And thou to be alone'—

'There let thy bleeding branch atone'

There let thy bleeding branch atone
For every torturing tear
Shall my young sins my sins alone
Be everlasting here?

Who bade thee keep that cursed name
A pledge for memory
As if Oblivion ever came
To breathe its bliss on me

As if through all the wildering maze
10 Of mad hours left behind
I once forgot the early days
That thou wouldst call to mind

'I see around me tombstones grey'

I see around me tombstones grey
Stretching their shadow far away.
Beneath the turf my footsteps tread
Lie low and lone the silent dead—
Beneath the turf – beneath the mould—
Forever dark, forever cold—
And my eyes cannot hold the tears
That memory hoards from vanished years
For Time and Death and Mortal pain
10 Give wounds that will not heal again—
Let me remember half the woe
I've seen and heard and felt below
And heaven itself – so pure and blest
Could never give my spirit rest—
Sweet land of light! thy children fair
Know nought akin to our despair—
Nor have they felt, nor can they tell
What tenants haunt each mortal cell
What gloomy guests we hold within—
20 Torments and madness, tears and sin!
Well – may they live in ecstasy
Their long eternity of joy;
At least we would not bring them down
With us to weep, with us to groan,
No – Earth would wish no other sphere
To taste her cup of sufferings drear;
She turns from Heaven a careless eye
And only mourns that *we* must die!
Ah mother, what shall comfort thee
30 In all this boundless misery?
To cheer our eager eyes a while
We see thee smile, how fondly smile!
But who reads not through that tender glow

Thy deep, unutterable woe?
Indeed no dazzling land above
Can cheat thee of thy children's love—
We all in life's departing shine
Our last dear longings blend with thine;
And struggle still, and strive to trace
40   With clouded gaze thy darling face
We would not leave our native home
For *any* world beyond the Tomb
No – rather on thy kindly breast
Let us be laid in lasting rest
Or waken but to share with thee
A mutual immortality—

The Philosopher

'Enough of thought, philosopher!
   Too long hast thou been dreaming
Unenlightened, in this chamber drear,
   While summer's sun is beaming!
Space-sweeping soul, what sad refrain
Concludes thy musings once again?

   '"Oh, for the time when I shall sleep
   Without identity,
   And never care how rain may steep,
10   Or snow may cover me!
No promised heaven, these wild desires,
   Could all, or half fulfil;
No threatened hell, with quenchless fires,
   Subdue this quenchless will!"'

'So said I, and still say the same;
  Still, to my death, will say—
Three gods, within this little frame,
  Are warring night and day;
Heaven could not hold them all, and yet
20 They all are held in me;
And must be mine till I forget
  My present entity!
Oh, for the time, when in my breast
  Their struggles will be o'er!
Oh, for the day, when I shall rest,
  And never suffer more!'

'I saw a spirit, standing, man,
  Where thou doth stand – an hour ago,
And round his feet three rivers ran,
30 Of equal depth, and equal flow—
A golden stream – and one like blood;
  And one like sapphire seemed to be;
But, where they joined their triple flood
  It tumbled in an inky sea.

The spirit sent his dazzling gaze
  Down through that ocean's gloomy night
Then, kindling all, with sudden blaze,
  The glad deep sparkled wide and bright—
White as the sun, far, far more fair
40 Than its divided sources were!'

'And even for that spirit, seer,
  I've watched and sought my life-time long;
Sought him in heaven, hell, earth, and air—
  An endless search, and always wrong!

Had I but seen his glorious eye
    Once light the clouds that wilder me,
I ne'er had raised this coward cry
    To cease to think, and cease to be;
I ne'er had called oblivion blest,
50   Nor, stretching eager hands to death,
Implored to change for senseless rest
    This sentient soul, this living breath—
Oh, let me die – that power and will
    Their cruel strife may close;
And conquered good, and conquering ill
    Be lost in one repose!'

Remembrance

Cold in the earth – and the deep snow piled above thee,
Far, far, removed, cold in the dreary grave!
Have I forgot, my only Love, to love thee,
Severed at last by Time's all-severing wave?

Now, when alone, do my thoughts no longer hover
Over the mountains, on that northern shore,
Resting their wings where heath and fern-leaves cover
Thy noble heart for ever, ever more?

Cold in the earth – and fifteen wild Decembers,
10 From those brown hills, have melted into spring:
Faithful, indeed, is the spirit that remembers
After such years of change and suffering!

Sweet Love of youth, forgive, if I forget thee,
While the world's tide is bearing me along;
Other desires and other hopes beset me,
Hopes which obscure, but cannot do thee wrong!

No later light has lightened up my heaven,
No second morn has ever shone for me;
All my life's bliss from thy dear life was given,
20   All my life's bliss is in the grave with thee.

But, when the days of golden dreams had perished,
And even Despair was powerless to destroy;
Then did I learn how existence could be cherished,
Strengthened, and fed without the aid of joy.

Then did I check the tears of useless passion—
Weaned my young soul from yearning after thine;
Sternly denied its burning wish to hasten
Down to that tomb already more than mine.

And, even yet, I dare not let it languish,
30   Dare not indulge in memory's rapturous pain;
Once drinking deep of that divinest anguish,
How could I seek the empty world again?

Death

Death! that struck when I was most confiding
In my certain faith of joy to be—
Strike again, Time's withered branch dividing
From the fresh root of Eternity!

Leaves, upon Time's branch, were growing brightly,
Full of sap, and full of silver dew;
Birds beneath its shelter gathered nightly;
Daily round its flowers the wild bees flew.

Sorrow passed, and plucked the golden blossom;
10   Guilt stripped off the foliage in its pride;

But, within its parent's kindly bosom,
Flowed for ever Life's restoring tide.

Little mourned I for the parted gladness,
For the vacant nest and silent song—
Hope was there, and laughed me out of sadness;
Whispering, 'Winter will not linger long!'

And, behold! with tenfold increase blessing,
Spring adorned the beauty-burdened spray;
Wind and rain and fervent heat, caressing,
20 Lavished glory on that second May!

High it rose – no winged grief could sweep it;
Sin was scared to distance with its shine;
Love, and its own life, had power to keep it
From all wrong – from every blight but thine!

Cruel Death! The young leaves droop and languish;
Evening's gentle air may still restore—
No! the morning sunshine mocks my anguish—
Time, for me, must never blossom more!

Strike it down, that other boughs may flourish
30 Where that perished sapling used to be;
Thus, at least, its mouldering corpse will nourish
That from which it sprung – Eternity.

Stars

Ah! why, because the dazzling sun
    Restored our Earth to joy,
Have you departed, every one,
    And left a desert sky?

All through the night, your glorious eyes
    Were gazing down in mine,
And with a full heart's thankful sighs,
    I blessed that watch divine.

I was at peace and drank your beams
10   As they were life to me;
And revelled in my changeful dreams,
    Like petrel on the sea.

Thought followed thought, star followed star,
    Through boundless regions, on;
While one sweet influence, near and far,
    Thrilled through, and proved us one!

Why did the morning dawn to break
    So great, so pure, a spell;
And scorch with fire, the tranquil cheek,
20   Where your cool radiance fell?

Blood-red, he rose, and, arrow-straight,
    His fierce beams struck my brow;
The soul of nature, sprang, elate,
    But *mine* sank sad and low!

My lids closed down, yet through their veil,
    I saw him, blazing, still,
And steep in gold the misty dale,
    And flash upon the hill.

I turned me to the pillow, then,
30   To call back night, and see
Your worlds of solemn light, again,
   Throb with my heart, and me!

It would not do – the pillow glowed,
   And glowed both roof and floor;
And birds sang loudly in the wood,
   And fresh winds shook the door;

The curtains waved, the wakened flies
   Were murmuring round my room,
Imprisoned there, till I should rise,
40   And give them leave to roam.

Oh, stars, and dreams, and gentle night;
   Oh, night and stars return!
And hide me from the hostile light,
   That does not warm, but burn;

That drains the blood of suffering men;
   Drinks tears, instead of dew;
Let me sleep through his blinding reign,
   And only wake with you!

The Prisoner
([A fragment of] A Fragment)

'He comes with western winds, with evening's wandering
   airs,
With that clear dusk of heaven that brings the thickest
   stars.
Winds take a pensive tone, and stars a tender fire,
And visions rise, and change, that kill me with desire.

'Desire for nothing known in my maturer years,
When Joy grew mad with awe, at counting future tears.
When, if my spirit's sky was full of flashes warm,
I knew not whence they came, from sun, or thunder storm.

'But, first, a hush of peace – a soundless calm descends;
10 The struggle of distress, and fierce impatience ends.
Mute music soothes my breast, unuttered harmony,
That I could never dream, till Earth was lost to me.

'Then dawns the Invisible; the Unseen its truth reveals;
My outward sense is gone, my inward essence feels:
Its wings are almost free – its home, its harbour found,
Measuring the gulf, it stoops, and dares the final bound.

'Oh, dreadful is the check – intense the agony—
When the ear begins to hear, and the eye begins to see;
When the pulse begins to throb, the brain to think again,
20 The soul to feel the flesh, and the flesh to feel the chain.

'Yet I would lose no sting, would wish no torture less,
The more that anguish racks, the earlier it will bless;
And robed in fires of hell, or bright with heavenly shine,
If it but herald death, the vision is divine!'

'No coward soul is mine'

No coward soul is mine
No trembler in the world's storm-troubled sphere
I see Heaven's glories shine
And Faith shines equal arming me from Fear

O God within my breast
Almighty ever-present Deity
Life, that in me hast rest
As I Undying Life, have power in thee

Vain are the thousand creeds
10 That move men's hearts, unutterably vain,
Worthless as withered weeds
Or idlest froth amid the boundless main

To waken doubt in one
Holding so fast by thy infinity
So surely anchored on
The steadfast rock of Immortality

With wide-embracing love
Thy spirit animates eternal years
Pervades and broods above,
20 Changes, sustains, dissolves, creates and rears

Though Earth and moon were gone
And suns and universes ceased to be
And thou wert left alone
Every Existence would exist in thee

There is not room for Death
Nor atom that his might could render void
Since thou art Being and Breath
And what thou art may never be destroyed

Introduction to Emily Dickinson

I must tell you about the character *of Amherst* wrote Mabel Todd, a newcomer to the town in 1881. *She has not been seen outside of her own house in 15 years . . . She writes finely, but no one* ever *sees her. (The Years and Hours of Emily Dickinson,* Jay Leyda, ed. vol 2, p. 357.) When Emily Dickinson was born in 1830, Amherst was a small town of fewer than three thousand people and her family were its most prominent citizens. She lived and died in the elegant house her grandfather built. She appears to have led a normal childhood, enjoyed a lively social life as a young woman, taken a full share of the domestic duties and only gradually withdrawn in her 30s into the seclusion for which she is famed. Her behaviour was commented on widely but her immediate family loved her and made no reference to finding her behaviour odd.

There appears to have been a crisis around 1861 when she was passionately and hopelessly in love and this may have happened again towards the end of her life. After her death, love letters addressed to 'Master' were discovered. The recipient is unknown nor whether the letters were ever sent. It may explain the feelings of rejection in her love poems *'The Soul selects her own Society'* (p.26), *'My life closed twice before its close'* (p.32) and *'That Love is all there is'* (p.33) and also in poems which do not immediately appear to be about love like *'Success is counted sweetest'* (p.23) and *'After great pain, a formal feeling comes'* (p.27).

Amherst lies in Massachusetts, New England, the part of America where the Puritans first settled. Dickinson was raised in a strict Calvinist tradition of moral accountability. Although she ceased to attend church and her attitude towards God is questioning, doubting, wryly accusing, as in *'Apparently with no surprise'* (p.32), her poetry remained deeply religious. One can hear the judging voice of puritan conscience in *'Over the fence'* (p.24) and *'The Soul selects her own Society'* (p.26). Many poems show the Calvinist virtues of rectitude, abstemiousness and pride in bearing troubles in solitude. Even her sparse style conveys a sense of puritanical moral restraint.

Dickinson was fascinated by the mysteriousness of death. Many of her poems register awe at its unknowable nature. See *'Safe in their*

Alabaster Chambers' (p.24), 'There's a certain Slant of light' (p.25), 'I heard a Fly buzz – when I died' (p.29) and 'Because I could not stop for Death' (p.30). We need to remember how prevalent loss and death were in the Nineteenth century, how often she had to endure the grief of losing people she loved.

Early in her life Dickinson tried to publish her work but with little success. Only five of nearly 50 poems she sent to magazines in the 1850s were accepted and these were altered, to her increasing annoyance, to make them more conventional. After these rebuffs she kept her writings private. In all, she wrote nearly 18 thousand poems, leaving many apparently unfinished with alternative words and no clear indication which, if any, was the favoured version. At some point in her life she copied many of them onto folded sheets of paper and threaded them together with string into bundles. Whether she had an order in mind, whether she was making her own books having despaired of publication, or whether she was simply tidying up, can never be known. Her later poems were found completely disorganized, written on scraps which she had to hand; brown paper bags; discarded envelopes; the back of a recipe; all in a sloping handwriting with interspersed dashes which have left editors with problems of how to punctuate them and which of the alternative versions to choose.

Elusiveness, indeterminacy, indecisiveness are the manner of Dickinson's writing, as they are its subject. She asks questions but evades answers, and the brevity and reticence of her poems invite different interpretations. Invariably the form she chooses is a simple, hymn-like lyric, deceptively at odds with the complexity of her language. Extreme compression makes her poems enigmatic. Single words hint at powerful, unstated meanings. Her ungrammatical, loosely punctuated, epigrammatic style, and casual, colloquial tone sound surprisingly modern and she is seen by feminist critics as subtly subversive. At a time when women were expected to deny their passions and remain silent about their powerlessness in a society which privileged men, her writing expressed the suffering this caused. Her teasing mockery is read as an attack on male authority and a protest at female repression. Funny and commanding by turns, Dickinson is now recognized as a major poet of striking originality.

'Success is counted sweetest'

Success is counted sweetest
By those who ne'er succeed.
To comprehend a nectar
Requires sorest need.

Not one of all the purple Host
Who took the Flag today
Can tell the definition
So clear of Victory

As he defeated – dying—
10 On whose forbidden ear
The distant strains of triumph
Burst agonized and clear!

'South Winds jostle them'

South Winds jostle them—
Bumblebees come—
Hover – hesitate—
Drink, and are gone—

Butterflies pause
On their passage Cashmere—
I – softly plucking,
Present them here!

'Safe in their Alabaster Chambers'

Safe in their Alabaster Chambers—
Untouched by Morning—
And untouched by Noon—
Lie the meek members of the Resurrection—
Rafter of Satin – and Roof of Stone!

Grand go the Years – in the Crescent – above them—
Worlds scoop their Arcs—
And Firmaments – row—
Diadems – drop – and Doges – surrender—
10 Soundless as dots – on a Disc of Snow—

version of 1861

'Over the fence'

Over the fence—
Strawberries – grow—
Over the fence—
I could climb – if I tried, I know—
Berries are nice!

But – if I stained my Apron—
God would certainly scold!
Oh, dear, – I guess if He were a Boy—
He'd – climb – if He could!

'There's a certain Slant of light'

There's a certain Slant of light,
Winter Afternoons—
That oppresses, like the Heft
Of Cathedral Tunes—

Heavenly Hurt, it gives us—
We can find no scar,
But internal difference,
Where the Meanings, are—

None may teach it – Any—
10 'Tis the Seal Despair—
An imperial affliction
Sent us of the Air—

When it comes, the Landscape listens—
Shadows – hold their breath—
When it goes, 'tis like the Distance
On the look of Death—

'I'm Nobody! Who are you?'

I'm Nobody! Who are you?
Are you – Nobody – too?
Then there's a pair of us!
Don't tell! they'd banish us – you know!

How dreary – to be – Somebody!
How public – like a Frog—
To tell your name – the livelong June—
To an admiring Bog!

'The Soul selects her own Society'

The Soul selects her own Society—
Then – shuts the Door—
To her divine Majority—
Present no more—

Unmoved – she notes the Chariots – pausing—
At her low Gate—
Unmoved – an Emperor be kneeling
Upon her Mat—

I've known her – from an ample nation—
10 Choose One—
Then – close the Valves of her attention—
Like Stone—

'A Bird came down the Walk'

A Bird came down the Walk—
He did not know I saw—
He bit an Angleworm in halves
And ate the fellow, raw,

And then he drank a Dew
From a convenient Grass—
And then hopped sidewise to the Wall
To let a Beetle pass—

He glanced with rapid eyes
10 That hurried all around—
They looked like frightened Beads, I thought—
He stirred his Velvet Head

Like one in danger, Cautious,
I offered him a Crumb
And he unrolled his feathers
And rowed him softer home—

Than Oars divide the Ocean,
Too silver for a seam—
Or Butterflies, off Banks of Noon
20 Leap, plashless as they swim.

'After great pain, a formal feeling comes'

After great pain, a formal feeling comes—
The Nerves sit ceremonious, like Tombs—
The stiff Heart questions was it He, that bore,
And Yesterday, or Centuries before?

The Feet, mechanical, go round—
Of Ground, or Air, or Ought—
A Wooden way
Regardless grown,
A Quartz contentment, like a stone—

10 This is the Hour of Lead—
Remembered, if outlived,
As Freezing persons, recollect the Snow—
First – Chill – then Stupor – then the letting go—

'We grow accustomed to the Dark'

We grow accustomed to the Dark—
When Light is put away—
As when the Neighbour holds the Lamp
To witness her Goodbye—

A Moment – We uncertain step
For newness of the night—
Then – fit our Vision to the Dark—
And meet the Road – erect—

And so of larger – Darknesses—
10 Those Evenings of the Brain—
When not a Moon disclose a sign—
Or Star – come out – within—

The Bravest – grope a little—
And sometimes hit a Tree
Directly in the Forehead—
But as they learn to see—

Either the Darkness alters—
Or something in the sight
Adjusts itself to Midnight—
20 And Life steps almost straight.

'I heard a Fly buzz – when I died'

I heard a Fly buzz – when I died—
The Stillness in the Room
Was like the Stillness in the Air—
Between the Heaves of Storm—

The Eyes around – had wrung them dry—
And Breaths were gathering firm
For that last Onset – when the King
Be witnessed – in the Room—

I willed my Keepsakes – Signed away
10 What portion of me be
Assignable – and then it was
There interposed a Fly—

With Blue – uncertain stumbling Buzz—
Between the light – and me—
And then the Windows failed – and then
I could not see to see—

'Because I could not stop for Death'

Because I could not stop for Death—
He kindly stopped for me—
The Carriage held but just Ourselves—
And Immortality.

We slowly drove – He knew no haste
And I had put away
My labour and my leisure too,
For His Civility—

We passed the School, where Children strove
10 At Recess – in the Ring—
We passed the Fields of Gazing Grain—
We passed the Setting Sun—

Or rather – He passed Us—
The Dews drew quivering and chill—
For only Gossamer, my Gown—
My Tippet – only Tulle—

We paused before a House that seemed
A Swelling of the Ground—
The Roof was scarcely visible—
20 The Cornice – in the Ground—

Since then – 'tis Centuries – and yet
Feels shorter than the Day
I first surmised the Horses' Heads
Were toward Eternity—

'Presentiment – is that long Shadow – on the Lawn'

Presentiment – is that long Shadow – on the Lawn—
Indicative that Suns go down—

The Notice to the startled Grass
That Darkness – is about to pass—

'Finding is the first Act'

Finding is the first Act
The second, loss,
Third, Expedition for
the 'Golden Fleece'

Fourth, no Discovery—
Fifth, no Crew—
Finally, no Golden Fleece—
Jason – sham – too.

'Immortal is an ample word'

Immortal is an ample word
When what we need is by
But when it leaves us for a time
'Tis a necessity.

Of Heaven above the firmest proof
We fundamental know
Except for its marauding Hand
It had been Heaven below.

'The Show is not the Show'

The Show is not the Show
But they that go—
Menagerie to me
My Neighbour be—
Fair Play—
Both went to see—

'Apparently with no surprise'

Apparently with no surprise
To any happy Flower
The Frost beheads it at its play—
In accidental power—
The blonde Assassin passes on—
The Sun proceeds unmoved
To measure off another Day
For an Approving God.

'The Pedigree of Honey'

The Pedigree of Honey
Does not concern the Bee—
A Clover, any time, to him,
Is Aristocracy—

version II

'My life closed twice before its close'

My life closed twice before its close;
It yet remains to see
If Immortality unveil
A third event to me,

So huge, so hopeless to conceive
As these that twice befell.
Parting is all we know of heaven,
And all we need of hell.

'To make a prairie it takes a clover and one bee'

To make a prairie it takes a clover and one bee,
One clover, and a bee,
And revery.
The revery alone will do,
If bees are few.

'Elysium is as far as to'

Elysium is as far as to
The very nearest Room
If in that Room a Friend await
Felicity or Doom—

What fortitude the Soul contains,
That it can so endure
The accent of a coming Foot—
The opening of a Door—

'That Love is all there is'

That Love is all there is,
Is all we know of Love;
It is enough, the freight should be
Proportioned to the groove.

Introduction to Sylvia Plath

> My childhood landscape was not land but the end of the land – the cold, salt, running hills of the Atlantic. I sometimes think my vision of the sea is the clearest thing I own. I pick it up, exile that I am . . . and in one wash of memory the colours deepen and gleam, the early world draws breath. ('Ocean 1212-W')

Sylvia Plath wrote about her earliest years in an essay called 'Ocean 1212-W' which was the code she dialled to phone her grandparents living further along the New England coast from her own seaside home in Winthrop, Massachusetts. The sounds and smells of the sea appear in her poetry and always they carry feelings of a wonderful strangeness which promises security as in *A Winter Ship* (p.38), *Morning Song* (p.44), and *Tulips* (p.45).

Plath was born in 1932. Her mother was Austrian, her father born in Poland, and both were German speaking. He was a professor of biology, a specialist on beekeeping who wrote a book entitled *Bumblebees and their Ways*. Her father died when she was nine years old after a long wasting disease *diabetes mellitus* which he had refused to have treated. After her father's death, her mother moved the family to Wellesley where she could work as a teacher.

> And this is how it stiffens, my vision of that seaside childhood. My father died, we moved inland. Whereupon those nine first years of my life sealed themselves off like a ship in a bottle – beautiful, inaccessible, obsolete. ('Ocean 1212-W')

Plath was an able, ambitious and unstable student who won many prizes, a scholarship to Smith College and, in 1953, a prestigious student guest editorship of *Mademoiselle*. Later that summer she attempted suicide and was found by chance, having lain unconscious for three days in the cellar of her home. She returned to Smith after a period in hospital, graduated and in 1955 went to England on a Fullbright Scholarship to study at Cambridge.

At Cambridge in 1956 Sylvia Plath met Ted Hughes. She was a bright, scholarship girl newly-arrived from America; he was a recent graduate who was already publishing poetry. In the small Cambridge world of student poets it was inevitable they would meet. What followed, in a matter of months, was one of the famous literary marriages of the Twentieth century. He went with her to America in 1957 where she taught for one year at Smith College before they decided to become full-time writers.

Plath's early poems were written slowly as she carefully tried to copy traditional patterns of rhyme and rhythm. Hughes described how she

> composed very slowly, consulting her Thesaurus and Dictionary for almost every word, putting a slow strong ring of ink around each word that attracted her. Her obsession with intricate rhyming and metrical schemes was part of the same process. Some of those early inventions of hers were almost perverse, with their bristling hurdles. (*Sylvia Plath* by Robyn Marsack, p.26)

The first poems in this selection belong to her experimental, apprenticeship period. In 1959, while the Hugheses were living in an artists' colony in Vermont, her style changed. Hughes wrote,

> she had never in her life improvised. The powers that compelled her to write so slowly had always been stronger than she was. But quite suddenly she found herself free to let herself drop, rather than inch over bridges of concepts. . . she now wrote at top speed, as one might write an urgent letter. From then on all her poems were written in this way. (*The Art of Sylvia Plath*, ed. Charles Newman, p.75)

The Hugheses returned to England, to London, late in 1959. Their daughter, Frieda, was born in 1960 and their son, Nicholas, in 1962. In 1961 they bought a small house in Devon where, like her father, Plath kept a beehive. In 1962 they separated and for a while she remained in Devon with the two children before moving back to London in the bitterly cold winter of 1962-3. There, on February 11, she committed suicide, gassing herself in the kitchen oven. In her final months, in a frenzy of poetic activity, Plath rose early each morning to write before the children woke. Her last poems for which she is most famed could not be more different from her early, laboured, carefully crafted pieces. Words and images spill out in vivid, free-wheeling lines and violent, inventive imagery. The facts of her life and death, and the controversy which continues to accompany any public discussion of it, make it difficult to read her poetry while withstanding the awareness of her terrible end. Nor is it clear that we should do so.

Ode for Ted

From under crunch of my man's boot
green oat-sprouts jut;
he names a lapwing, starts rabbits in a rout
legging it most nimble
to sprigged hedge of bramble,
stalks red fox, shrewd stoat.

Loam-humps, he says, moles shunt
up from delved worm-haunt;
blue fur, moles have; hefting chalk-hulled flint
10   he with rock splits open
knobbed quartz; flayed colours ripen
rich, brown, sudden in sunglint.

For his least look, scant acres yield:
each finger-furrowed field
heaves forth stalk, leaf, fruit-nubbed emerald;
bright grain sprung so rarely
he hauls to his will early;
at his hand's staunch hest, birds build.

Ringdoves roost well within his wood,
20   shirr songs to suit which mood
he saunters in; how but most glad
could be this adam's woman
when all earth his words do summon
leaps to laud such man's blood!

Black Rook in Rainy Weather

On the stiff twig up there
Hunches a wet black rook
Arranging and rearranging its feathers in the rain.
I do not expect a miracle

Or an accident
To set the sight on fire
In my eye, nor seek
Any more in the desultory weather some design,
But let spotted leaves fall as they fall,
10 Without ceremony, or portent.

Although, I admit, I desire,
Occasionally, some backtalk
From the mute sky, I can't honestly complain:
A certain minor light may still
Lean incandescent

Out of kitchen table or chair
As if a celestial burning took
Possession of the most obtuse objects now and then—
Thus hallowing an interval
20 Otherwise inconsequent

By bestowing largesse, honour,
One might say love. At any rate, I now walk
Wary (for it could happen
Even in this dull, ruinous landscape); skeptical,
Yet politic; ignorant

Of whatever angel may choose to flare
Suddenly at my elbow. I only know that a rook
Ordering its black feathers can so shine
As to seize my senses, haul
30 My eyelids up, and grant

A brief respite from fear
Of total neutrality. With luck,
Trekking stubborn through this season
Of fatigue, I shall
Patch together a content

Of sorts. Miracles occur,
If you care to call those spasmodic
Tricks of radiance miracles. The wait's begun again,
The long wait for the angel,
40 For that rare, random descent.

A Winter Ship

At this wharf there are no grand landings to speak of.
Red and orange barges list and blister
Shackled to the dock, outmoded, gaudy,
And apparently indestructible.
The sea pulses under a skin of oil.

A gull holds his pose on a shanty ridgepole,
Riding the tide of the wind, steady
As wood and formal, in a jacket of ashes,
The whole flat harbour anchored in
10 The round of his yellow eye-button.

A blimp swims up like a day-moon or tin
Cigar over his rink of fishes.
The prospect is dull as an old etching.
They are unloading three barrels of little crabs.
The pier pilings seem about to collapse

And with them that rickety edifice
Of warehouses, derricks, smokestacks and bridges
In the distance. All around us the water slips
And gossips in its loose vernacular,
20   Ferrying the smells of dead cod and tar.

Farther out, the waves will be mouthing icecakes—
A poor month for park-sleepers and lovers.
Even our shadows are blue with cold.
We wanted to see the sun come up
And are met, instead, by this iceribbed ship,

Bearded and blown, an albatross of frost,
Relic of tough weather, every winch and stay
Encased in a glassy pellicle.
The sun will diminish it soon enough:
30   Each wave-tip glitters like a knife.

Two Views of a Cadaver Room

I

The day she visited the dissecting room
They had four men laid out, black as burnt turkey,
Already half unstrung. A vinegary fume
Of the death vats clung to them;
The white-smocked boys started working.
The head of his cadaver had caved in,
And she could scarcely make out anything
In that rubble of skull plates and old leather.
A sallow piece of string held it together.

10   In their jars the snail-nosed babies moon and glow.
He hands her the cut-out heart like a cracked heirloom.

II

In Brueghel's panorama of smoke and slaughter
Two people only are blind to the carrion army:
He, afloat in the sea of her blue satin
Skirts, sings in the direction
Of her bare shoulder, while she bends,
Fingering a leaflet of music, over him,
Both of them deaf to the fiddle in the hands
Of the death's-head shadowing their song.
20   These Flemish lovers flourish; not for long.

Yet desolation, stalled in paint, spares the little country
Foolish, delicate, in the lower right hand corner.

Metaphors

I'm a riddle in nine syllables,
An elephant, a ponderous house,
A melon strolling on two tendrils.
O red fruit, ivory, fine timbers!
This loaf's big with its yeasty rising.
Money's new-minted in this fat purse.
I'm a means, a stage, a cow in calf.
I've eaten a bag of green apples,
Boarded the train there's no getting off.

The Colossus

I shall never get you put together entirely,
Pieced, glued, and properly jointed.
Mule-bray, pig-grunt and bawdy cackles
Proceed from your great lips.
It's worse than a barnyard.

Perhaps you consider yourself an oracle,
Mouthpiece of the dead, or of some god or other.
Thirty years now I have laboured
To dredge the silt from your throat.
10 I am none the wiser.

Scaling little ladders with gluepots and pails of Lysol
I crawl like an ant in mourning
Over the weedy acres of your brow
To mend the immense skull-plates and clear
The bald, white tumuli of your eyes.

A blue sky out of the Oresteia
Arches above us. O father, all by yourself
You are pithy and historical as the Roman Forum.
I open my lunch on a hill of black cypress.
20   Your fluted bones and acanthine hair are littered

In their old anarchy to the horizon-line.
It would take more than a lightning-stroke
To create such a ruin.
Nights, I squat in the cornucopia
Of your left ear, out of the wind,

Counting the red stars and those of plum-colour.
The sun rises under the pillar of your tongue.
My hours are married to shadow.
No longer do I listen for the scrape of a keel
30   On the blank stones of the landing.

Mushrooms

Overnight, very
Whitely, discreetly,
Very quietly

Our toes, our noses
Take hold on the loam,
Acquire the air.

Nobody sees us,
Stops us, betrays us;
The small grains make room.

10   Soft fists insist on
Heaving the needles,
The leafy bedding,

Even the paving.
Our hammers, our rams,
Earless and eyeless,

Perfectly voiceless,
Widen the crannies,
Shoulder through holes. We

Diet on water,
20   On crumbs of shadow,
Bland-mannered, asking

Little or nothing.
So many of us!
So many of us!

We are shelves, we are
Tables, we are meek,
We are edible,

Nudgers and shovers
In spite of ourselves.
30   Our kind multiplies:

We shall by morning
Inherit the earth.
Our foot's in the door.

You're

Clownlike, happiest on your hands,
Feet to the stars, and moon-skulled,
Gilled like a fish. A common-sense
Thumbs-down on the dodo's mode.
Wrapped up in yourself like a spool,
Trawling your dark as owls do.
Mute as a turnip from the Fourth
Of July to All Fools' Day,
O high-riser, my little loaf.

10 Vague as fog and looked for like mail.
Farther off than Australia.
Bent-backed Atlas, our travelled prawn.
Snug as a bud and at home
Like a sprat in a pickle jug.
A creel of eels, all ripples.
Jumpy as a Mexican bean.
Right, like a well-done sum.
A clean slate, with your own face on.

Morning Song

Love set you going like a fat gold watch.
The midwife slapped your footsoles, and your bald cry
Took its place among the elements.

Our voices echo, magnifying your arrival. New statue.
In a drafty museum, your nakedness
Shadows our safety. We stand round blankly as walls.

I'm no more your mother
Than the cloud that distils a mirror to reflect its own slow
Effacement at the wind's hand.

10 All night your moth-breath
Flickers among the flat pink roses. I wake to listen:
A far sea moves in my ear.

One cry, and I stumble from bed, cow-heavy and floral
In my Victorian nightgown.
Your mouth opens clean as a cat's. The window square

Whitens and swallows its dull stars. And now you try
Your handful of notes;
The clear vowels rise like balloons.

Tulips

The tulips are too excitable, it is winter here.
Look how white everything is, how quiet, how snowed-in.
I am learning peacefulness, lying by myself quietly
As the light lies on these white walls, this bed, these hands.
I am nobody; I have nothing to do with explosions.
I have given my name and my day-clothes up to the nurses
And my history to the anaesthetist and my body to
surgeons.

They have propped my head between the pillow and the
sheet-cuff
Like an eye between two white lids that will not shut.
10 Stupid pupil, it has to take everything in.
The nurses pass and pass, they are no trouble,

They pass the way gulls pass inland in their white caps,
Doing things with their hands, one just the same as
    another,
So it is impossible to tell how many there are.

My body is a pebble to them, they tend it as water
Tends to the pebbles it must run over, smoothing them
    gently.
They bring me numbness in their bright needles, they bring
    me sleep.
Now I have lost myself I am sick of baggage—
My patent leather overnight case like a black pillbox,
20 My husband and child smiling out of the family photo;
Their smiles catch onto my skin, little smiling hooks.

I have let things slip, a thirty-year-old cargo boat
Stubbornly hanging on to my name and address.
They have swabbed me clear of my loving associations.
Scared and bare on the green plastic-pillowed trolley
I watched my teaset, my bureaus of linen, my books
Sink out of sight, and the water went over my head.
I am a nun now, I have never been so pure.

I didn't want any flowers, I only wanted
30 To lie with my hands turned up and be utterly empty.
How free it is, you have no idea how free—
The peacefulness is so big it dazes you,
And it asks nothing, a name tag, a few trinkets.
It is what the dead close on, finally; I imagine them
Shutting their mouths on it, like a Communion tablet.

The tulips are too red in the first place, they hurt me.
Even through the gift paper I could hear them breathe
Lightly, through their white swaddlings, like an awful baby.
Their redness talks to my wound, it corresponds.

40 They are subtle: they seem to float, though they weigh me
        down,
    Upsetting me with their sudden tongues and their colour,
    A dozen red lead sinkers round my neck.

    Nobody watched me before, now I am watched.
    The tulips turn to me, and the window behind me
    Where once a day the light slowly widens and slowly thins,
    And I see myself, flat, ridiculous, a cut-paper shadow
    Between the eye of the sun and the eyes of the tulips,
    And I have no face, I have wanted to efface myself.
    The vivid tulips eat my oxygen.

50 Before they came the air was calm enough,
    Coming and going, breath by breath, without any fuss.
    Then the tulips filled it up like a loud noise.
    Now the air snags and eddies round them the way a river
    Snags and eddies round a sunken rust-red engine.
    They concentrate my attention, that was happy
    Playing and resting without committing itself.

    The walls, also, seem to be warming themselves.
    The tulips should be behind bars like dangerous animals;
    They are opening like the mouth of some great African
        cat,
60 And I am aware of my heart: it opens and closes
    Its bowl of red blooms out of sheer love of me.
    The water I taste is warm and salt, like the sea,
    And comes from a country far away as health.

The Arrival of the Bee Box

I ordered this, this clean wood box
Square as a chair and almost too heavy to lift.
I would say it was the coffin of a midget
Or a square baby
Were there not such a din in it.

The box is locked, it is dangerous.
I have to live with it overnight
And I can't keep away from it.
There are no windows, so I can't see what is in there.
10   There is only a little grid, no exit.

I put my eye to the grid.
It is dark, dark,
With the swarmy feeling of African hands
Minute and shrunk for export,
Black on black, angrily clambering.

How can I let them out?
It is the noise that appals me most of all,
The unintelligible syllables.
It is like a Roman mob,
20   Small, taken one by one, but my god, together!

I lay my ear to furious Latin.
I am not a Caesar.
I have simply ordered a box of maniacs.
They can be sent back.
They can die, I need feed them nothing, I am the owner.

I wonder how hungry they are.
I wonder if they would forget me
If I just undid the locks and stood back and turned into a
    tree.
There is the laburnum, its blond colonnades,
30 And the petticoats of the cherry.

They might ignore me immediately
In my moon suit and funeral veil.
I am no source of honey
So why should they turn on me?
Tomorrow I will be sweet God, I will set them free.

The box is only temporary.

The Applicant

First, are you our sort of a person?
Do you wear
A glass eye, false teeth or a crutch,
A brace or a hook,
Rubber breasts or a rubber crotch,

Stitches to show something's missing? No, no? Then
How can we give you a thing?
Stop crying.
Open your hand.
10 Empty? Empty. Here is a hand

To fill it and willing
To bring teacups and roll away headaches
And do whatever you tell it.
Will you marry it?
It is guaranteed

To thumb shut your eyes at the end
And dissolve of sorrow.
We make new stock from the salt.
I notice you are stark naked.
20 How about this suit—

Black and stiff, but not a bad fit.
Will you marry it?
It is waterproof, shatterproof, proof
Against fire and bombs through the roof.
Believe me, they'll bury you in it.

Now your head, excuse me, is empty.
I have the ticket for that.
Come here, sweetie, out of the closet.
Well, what do you think of *that?*
30 Naked as paper to start

But in twenty-five years she'll be silver,
In fifty, gold.
A living doll, everywhere you look.
It can sew, it can cook,
It can talk, talk, talk.

It works, there is nothing wrong with it.
You have a hole, it's a poultice.
You have an eye, it's an image.
My boy, it's your last resort.
40 Will you marry it, marry it, marry it.

Daddy

You do not do, you do not do
Any more, black shoe
In which I have lived like a foot
For thirty years, poor and white,
Barely daring to breathe or Achoo.

Daddy, I have had to kill you.
You died before I had time—
Marble-heavy, a bag full of God,
Ghastly statue with one grey toe
10 Big as a Frisco seal

And a head in the freakish Atlantic
Where it pours bean green over blue
In the waters off beautiful Nauset.
I used to pray to recover you.
Ach, du.

In the German tongue, in the Polish town
Scraped flat by the roller
Of wars, wars, wars.
But the name of the town is common.
20 My Polack friend

Says there are a dozen or two.
So I never could tell where you
Put your foot, your root,
I never could talk to you.
The tongue stuck in my jaw.

It stuck in a barb wire snare.
Ich, ich, ich, ich,
I could hardly speak.
I thought every German was you.
30 And the language obscene

An engine, an engine
Chuffing me off like a Jew.
A Jew to Dachau, Auschwitz, Belsen.
I began to talk like a Jew.
I think I may well be a Jew.

The snows of the Tyrol, the clear beer of Vienna
Are not very pure or true.
With my gypsy ancestress and my weird luck
And my Taroc pack and my Taroc pack
40 I may be a bit of a Jew.

I have always been scared of *you*,
With your Luftwaffe, your gobbledygoo.
And your neat moustache
And your Aryan eye, bright blue.
Panzer-man, panzer-man, O You—

Not God but a swastika
So black no sky could squeak through.
Every woman adores a Fascist,
The boot in the face, the brute
50 Brute heart of a brute like you.

You stand at the blackboard, daddy,
In the picture I have of you,
A cleft in your chin instead of your foot
But no less a devil for that, no not
Any less the black man who

Bit my pretty red heart in two.
I was ten when they buried you.
At twenty I tried to die
And get back, back, back to you.
60   I thought even the bones would do.

But they pulled me out of the sack,
And they stuck me together with glue.
And then I knew what to do.
I made a model of you,
A man in black with a Meinkampf look

And a love of the rack and the screw.
And I said I do, I do.
So daddy, I'm finally through.
The black telephone's off at the root,
70   The voices just can't worm through.

If I've killed one man, I've killed two—
The vampire who said he was you
And drank my blood for a year,
Seven years, if you want to know.
Daddy, you can lie back now.

There's a stake in your fat black heart
And the villagers never liked you.
They are dancing and stamping on you.
They always *knew* it was you.
80   Daddy, daddy, you bastard, I'm through.

Lady Lazarus

I have done it again.
One year in every ten
I manage it—

A sort of walking miracle, my skin
Bright as a Nazi lampshade,
My right foot

A paperweight,
My face a featureless, fine
Jew linen.

10   Peel off the napkin
O my enemy
Do I terrify?—

The nose, the eye pits, the full set of teeth?
The sour breath
Will vanish in a day.

Soon, soon the flesh
The grave cave ate will be
At home on me

And I a smiling woman.
20   I am only thirty.
And like the cat I have nine times to die.

This is Number Three.
What a trash
To annihilate each decade.

What a million filaments.
The peanut-crunching crowd
Shoves in to see

Them unwrap me hand and foot—
The big strip tease.
30 Gentlemen, ladies

These are my hands
My knees.
I may be skin and bone,

Nevertheless, I am the same, identical woman.
The first time it happened I was ten.
It was an accident.

The second time I meant
To last it out and not come back at all.
I rocked shut

40 As a seashell.
They had to call and call
And pick the worms off me like sticky pearls.

Dying
Is an art, like everything else.
I do it exceptionally well.

I do it so it feels like hell.
I do it so it feels real.
I guess you could say I've a call.

It's easy enough to do it in a cell.
50 It's easy enough to do it and stay put.
It's the theatrical

Comeback in broad day
To the same place, the same face, the same brute
Amused shout:

'A miracle!'
That knocks me out.
There is a charge

For the eyeing of my scars, there is a charge
For the hearing of my heart—
60 It really goes.

And there is a charge, a very large charge
For a word or a touch
Or a bit of blood

Or a piece of my hair or my clothes.
So, so, Herr Doktor.
So, Herr Enemy.

I am your opus,
I am your valuable,
The pure gold baby

70 That melts to a shriek.
I turn and burn.
Do not think I underestimate your great concern.

Ash, ash—
You poke and stir.
Flesh, bone, there is nothing there—

A cake of soap,
A wedding ring,
A gold filling.

Herr God, Herr Lucifer
80   Beware
Beware.

Out of the ash
I rise with my red hair
And I eat men like air.

Balloons

Since Christmas they have lived with us,
Guileless and clear,
Oval soul-animals,
Taking up half the space,
Moving and rubbing on the silk

Invisible air drifts,
Giving a shriek and pop
When attacked, then scooting to rest, barely trembling.
Yellow cathead, blue fish—
10   Such queer moons we live with

Instead of dead furniture!
Straw mats, white walls
And these travelling
Globes of thin air, red, green,
Delighting

The heart like wishes or free
Peacocks blessing
Old ground with a feather
Beaten in starry metals.
20   Your small

Brother is making
His balloon squeak like a cat.
Seeming to see
A funny pink world he might eat on the other side of it,
He bites,

Then sits
Back, fat jug
Contemplating a world clear as water.
A red
30   Shred in his little fist.

Edge

The woman is perfected.
Her dead

Body wears the smile of accomplishment,
The illusion of a Greek necessity

Flows in the scrolls of her toga,
Her bare

Feet seem to be saying:
We have come so far, it is over.

Each dead child coiled, a white serpent,
10 One at each little

Pitcher of milk, now empty.
She has folded

Them back into her body as petals
Of a rose close when the garden

Stiffens and odours bleed
From the sweet, deep throats of the night flower.

The moon has nothing to be sad about,
Staring from her hood of bone.

She is used to this sort of thing.
20 Her blacks crackle and drag.

Introduction by Elizabeth Jennings

I give poetry readings fairly often and am usually asked a lot of questions afterwards about what the poems spring from, how they work, their craftsmanship and discipline and much else. I more often than not feel a rapport, an established link. A question I must try to answer teaches me things about my own work. In other words, readings become creative functions.

So, very often dialogue is made, a two-way traffic begins. Poems are something you make, and later, when you feel a little confidence about them, they are dialogues. You do not think of publication while you are actually writing but you do hope for publication and at a later hearing monologues are usually boring and often untrue. A poem should speak for itself, should attempt to reach the mind and heart of a reader. The last thing a poem should need is a dictionary, let alone analyses, or explications.

But, of course, there are always exceptions to this rule. The great pioneers of modern English poetry such as T. S. Eliot of *The Waste Land* will always be intractable and arcane. Like Ezra Pound, Eliot led the way, he did not build bridges or set out all the road-signs. Poets who start by being difficult will generally end by being lucid.

My own poetry, like that of many of my generation, such as Thom Gunn and Philip Larkin, is lyrical and speaks directly. That does not mean that it cannot handle large themes, such as love, death, and suffering. In the last twenty years, I have extended my own range of subject-matter, I have also evolved a long loose line which grows out of the iambic pentameter. Without realizing it, I found that these lines had a great deal of assonance and alliteration in them. Over the years I have, I believe, gradually ceased to use the poetic 'I'. My poems are more concerned with 'we' and 'they' and 'he' or 'she'.

In the last few years, I have written a good deal about my childhood. It has become quite suddenly most brilliantly alive for me. I have written poems on a religious theme from my early days but now such poems have become journeys of discovery. Poetry seems so perfectly adapted to the great Christian themes and events. I still write vers libre at times and also what I call 'poems of magic' such as the greatest poets have produced. I am thinking of Keats' *La Belle Dame Sans Merci* and Coleridge's *Kubla Khan.*

Maybe this is why I love the intensely individual work of Klee, Chagall, and Henri Rousseau. I love looking at pictures and am a frequent visitor to the cinema.

In all my poetry I owe most to W. H. Auden, a great poet of extraordinarily varied thematic and formal skill. He has taught me to use the adjective which seems just right but which is also surprising. It can jerk the reader awake!

The Climbers

To the cold peak without their careful women
(Who watching children climbing into dreams
Go dispossessed at home). The mountain moves
Away at every climb and steps are hard
Frozen along the glacier. Every man
Tied to the rope constructs himself alone.

And not the summit reached nor any pole
Touched is the wished embrace, but still to move
And as the mountain climbs to see it whole
10   And each mind's landscape growing more complete
As sinews strain and all the muscles knot.

One at the peak is small. His disappointment
The coloured flag flown at the lonely top,
And all the valley's motive grown obscure.
He envies the large toilers halfway there
Who still possess the mountain by desire
And, not arriving, dream in no resentment.

Kings

You send an image hurrying out of doors
When you depose a king and seize his throne:
You exile symbols when you take by force.

And even if you say the power's your own.
That you are your own hero, your own king
You will not wear the meaning of the crown.

The power a ruler has is how men bring
Their thoughts to bear upon him, how their minds
Construct the grandeur from the simple thing.

10 And kings prevented from their proper ends
Make a deep lack in men's imaginings;
Heroes are nothing without worshipping,

Will not diminish into lovers, friends.

Beyond Possession

Our images withdraw, the rose returns
To what it was before we looked at it.
We lift our looks from where the water runs
And it's pure river once again, we write
No emblems on the trees. A way begins
Of living where we have no need to beat
The petals down to get the scent of rose
Or sign our features where the water goes.

All is itself. Each man himself entire,
10   Not even plucking out his thought, not even
Bringing a tutored wilfulness to bear
Upon the rose, the water. Each has given
Essence of water back to itself, essence of flower,
Till he is yoked to his own heart and driven
Inward to find a private kind of peace
And not a mind reflecting his own face.

Yet must go deeper still, must move to love
Where thought is free to let the water ride,
Is liberal to the rose giving it life
20   And setting even its own shadow aside;
Till flower and water blend with freedom of
Passion that does not close them in and hide
Their deepest natures; but the heart is strong
To beat with rose and river in one song.

For a Child Born Dead

What ceremony can we fit
You into now? If you had come
Out of a warm and noisy room
To this, there'd be an opposite
For us to know you by. We could
Imagine you in lively mood

And then look at the other side,
The mood drawn out of you, the breath
Defeated by the power of death.
10   But we have never seen you stride
Ambitiously the world we know.
You could not come and yet you go.

But there is nothing now to mar
Your clear refusal of our world.
Not in our memories can we mould
You or distort your character.
Then all our consolation is
That grief can be as pure as this.

Mirrors

Was it a mirror then across a room,
A crowded room of parties where the smoke
Rose to the ceiling with the talk? The glass
Stared back at me a half-familiar face
Yet something hoped for. When at last you came
It was as if the distant mirror spoke.

That loving ended as all self-love ends
And teaches us that only fair-grounds have
The right to show us halls of mirrors where
10   In every place we look we see our stare
Taunting our own identities. But love
Perceives without a mirror in the hands.

In the Night

Out of my window late at night I gape
And see the stars but do not watch them really,
And hear the trains but do not listen clearly;
Inside my mind I turn about to keep
Myself awake, yet am not there entirely.
Something of me is out in the dark landscape.

How much am I then what I think, how much what I feel?
How much the eye that seems to keep stars straight?
Do I control what I can contemplate
10 Or is it my vision that's amenable?
I turn in my mind, my mind is a room whose wall
I can see the top of but never completely scale.

All that I love is, like the night, outside,
Good to be gazed at, looking as if it could
With a simple gesture be brought inside my head
Or in my heart. But my thoughts about it divide
Me from my object. Now deep in my bed
I turn and the world turns on the other side.

Choices

Inside the room I see the table laid,
Four chairs, a patch of light the lamp has made

And people there so deep in tenderness
They could not speak a word of happiness.

Outside I stand and see my shadow drawn
Lengthening the clipped grass of the cared-for lawn.

Above, their roof holds half the sky behind.
A dog barks bringing distances to mind.

Comfort, I think, or safety then, or both?
10 I warm the cold air with my steady breath.

They have designed a way to live and I,
Clothed in confusion, set their choices by:

Though sometimes one looks up and sees me there,
Alerts his shadow, pushes back his chair

And, opening windows wide, looks out at me
And close past words we stare. It seems that he

Urges my darkness, dares it to be freed
Into that room. We need each other's need.

Fountain

Let it disturb no more at first
Than the hint of a pool predicted far in a forest,
Or a sea so far away that you have to open
Your window to hear it.
Think of it then as elemental, as being
Necessity,
Not for a cup to be taken to it and not
For lips to linger or eye to receive itself
Back in reflection, simply
10 As water the patient moon persuades and stirs.

And then step closer,
Imagine rivers you might indeed embark on,
Waterfalls where you could
Silence an afternoon by staring but never
See the same tumult twice.
Yes come out of the narrow street and enter
The full piazza. Come where the noise compels.
Statues are bowing down to the breaking air.

Observe it there – the fountain, too fast for shadows,
20 Too wild for the lights which illuminate it to hold,
Even a moment, an ounce of water back;
Stare at such prodigality and consider
It is the elegance here, it is the taming,
The keeping fast in a thousand flowering sprays,
That builds this energy up but lets the watchers
See in that stress an image of utter calm,
A stillness there. It is how we must have felt
Once at the edge of some perpetual stream,
Fearful of touching, bringing no thirst at all,
30 Panicked by no perception of ourselves
But drawing the water down to the deepest wonder.

My Grandmother

She kept an antique shop – or it kept her.
Among Apostle spoons and Bristol glass,
The faded silks, the heavy furniture,
She watched her own reflection in the brass
Salvers and silver bowls, as if to prove
Polish was all, there was no need of love.

And I remember how I once refused
To go out with her, since I was afraid.
It was perhaps a wish not to be used
10   Like antique objects. Though she never said
That she was hurt, I still could feel the guilt
Of that refusal, guessing how she felt.

Later, too frail to keep a shop, she put
All her best things in one long narrow room.
The place smelt old, of things too long kept shut,
The smell of absences where shadows come
That can't be polished. There was nothing then
To give her own reflection back again.

And when she died I felt no grief at all,
20   Only the guilt of what I once refused.
I walked into her room among the tall
Sideboards and cupboards – things she never used
But needed; and no finger-marks were there,
Only the new dust falling through the air.

World I Have Not Made

I have sometimes thought how it would have been
if I had had to create the whole thing myself—
my life certainly but also something else;
I mean a world which I could inhabit freely,
ideas, objects, everything prepared;
not ideas simply as Plato knew them,
shadows of shadows, but more like furniture,
something to move around and live in,
something I had made. But still there would be
10 all that I hadn't made – animals, stars,
tides tugging against me, moon uncaring,
and the trying to love without reciprocity.
All this is here still. It is hard, hard,
even with free faith outlooking boundaries,
to come to terms with obvious suffering.
I live in a world I have not created
inward or outward. There is a sweetness
in willing surrender: I trail my ideas
behind great truths. My ideas are like shadows
20 and sometimes I consider how it would have been
to create a credo, objects, ideas
and then to live with them. I can understand
when tides most tug and the moon is remote
and the trapped wild beast is one with its shadow,
how even great faith leaves room for abysses
and the taut mind turns to its own requirings.

The Diamond Cutter

Not what the light will do but how he shapes it
And what particular colours it will bear,

And something of the climber's concentration
Seeing the white peak, setting the right foot there.

Not how the sun was plausible at morning
Nor how it was distributed at noon,

And not how much the single stone could show
But rather how much brilliance it would shun;

Simply a paring down, a cleaving to
10   One object, as the star-gazer who sees

One single comet polished by its fall
Rather than countless, untouched galaxies.

Greek Statues

These I have never touched but only looked at.
If you could say that stillness meant surrender
These are surrendered,
Yet their large audacious gestures signify surely
Remonstrance, reprisal? What have they left to lose
But the crumbling away by rain or time? Defiance
For them is a dignity, a declaration.

Odd how one wants to touch not simply stare,
To run one's finger over the flanks and arms.
10 Not to possess, rather to be possessed.
Bronze is bright to the eye but under the hands
Is cool and calming. Gods into silent metal:

To stone also, not to the palpable flesh.
Incarnations are elsewhere and more human,
Something concerning us; but these are other.
It is as if something infinite, remote
Permitted intrusion. It is as if these blind eyes
Exposed a landscape precious with grapes and olives:
And our probing hands move not to grasp but praise.

The Interrogator

He is always right.
However you prevaricate or question his motives,
Whatever you say to excuse yourself
He is always right.

He always has an answer;
It may be a question that hurts to hear.
It may be a sentence that makes you flinch.
He always has an answer.

He always knows best.
10 He can tell you why you disliked your father,
He can make your purest motive seem aggressive.
He always knows best.

He can always find words.
While you fumble to feel for your own position
Or stammer out words that are not quite accurate,
He can always find words.

And if you accuse him
He is glad you have lost your temper with him.
He can find the motive, give you a reason
20 If you accuse him.

And if you covered his mouth with your hand,
Pinned him down to his smooth desk chair,
You would be doing just what he wishes.
His silence would prove that he was right.

Remembering Fireworks

Always as if for the first time we watch
The fireworks as if no one had ever
Done this before, made shapes, signs,
Cut diamonds on air, sent up stars
Nameless, imperious. And in the falling
Of fire, the spent rocket, there is a kind
Of nostalgia as normally only attaches
To things long known and lost. Such an absence,
Such emptiness of sky the fireworks leave
10 After their festival. We, fumbling
For words of love, remember the rockets.
The spinning wheels, the sudden diamonds,
And say with delight 'Yes, like that, like that.'
Oh and the air is full of falling
Stars surrendered. We search for a sign.

Legacies and Language

I have learnt my tongue
From cities that are neighbourly and near water,
Where wren or rook or sea-gull lance the air,
Where the land is flat and above it the sea sows its salt.
That was my first home,
Born in Boston, Lincolnshire,
Reared in a flat land of sugar-beet and tulips
But with mind attuned to the tides, the heart ready for
    journeys
I learnt the song of storms and ships at anchor
10 Where the tide governs the mind. Till I was six
These were legacies but my inheritance then
Came from the damp, soft valley of Oxford's Thames
Where the air is slow and easily misted, where minds
Cogitate, think long and companionably but do not draw
Easy conclusions. For rest, for recreation,
The bells of the churches oddly ring for services
Which are not so often attended. I was a cross-breed also,
Christened to Catholic Christianity, oiled and marked
With the name of Rome on my lips. I learnt the Latin
20 Of stone and pillar. The Greek was soft and persuasive
But Rome spread out the glory of the Renaissance
Colours and light, huge marble presences,
Raphael's frescos filling rooms in the Vatican
And Raphael, loved by all and dying young,
Brought all Rome out to conduct him to the Pantheon.
But Rome became neighbourly when I was out of my teens
And ripe for renewal of vows. The child's belief
Had to argue with flesh and blood, must vanish, must go
    underground
To the catacombs and the dark long memories there
30 And doubt and be afraid but came up suddenly
Into the bold Baroque, into the city of artifice

Where a square is a circle, Bernini lays down his columns
And in the fountains between them and in all Rome's
    fountains
I learnt the sound of water, it versed and instructed me,
Took over all my English lyric sense
And gave it deeper roots and wider branches
And now, though unvisited for a number of years,
Rome does not haunt but holds me, is a presence,
Gives me a landscape utterly unlike Oxford's
40 And therefore a conflict that ends in the dance of phrases.
Latin and Anglo-Saxon are not estranged
But sing together as language lives and changes—
The Saxon, the Roman, the Norman, the modern with all
Its trends and touches. The dance becomes more elaborate
And carries me on and on. It is like love
That bears you beyond the guesswork of first rejoicing
And sets you on a rock facing the sea,
Your hand in another's or in the tide's or in rock-pools,
All's passionate and remote, personal yet also general,
50 In fact a system of rites, of comings-together
Where poetry is the common language of dreams
But also of love and its profound legislation.

Thinking of Descartes

I can see him cogitating, watch him with
A candle-flame. There's Descartes by himself
And by himself he's back where Aristotle,
Aquinas too began.
The crucial question is the same, 'How much,
If anything, can our minds know?' The quest
Was pure and selfless, spiritual also
As any human wish can be. Descartes
Conjured a naughty spirit who might lead
10 The mind astray, and then he asked himself
How he could tell a dream from waking thought,
When was he sure he was awake? At last
On those pure peaks where speculation shows
Ideas can be pinned down at last, Descartes
Thought how he thought of God, a greater Being
Held in his mind, thus greater than his thought
But still the vexing query was not answered
Until, perhaps in homely and slow ways
Or, and it seems more likely, in a dazzle
20 Of recognition, Descartes saw that thought,
Himself a thinker, proved he was created,
Authenticated by the famous slogan
'I think therefore I am'. For most of us
This is sufficient. Not for this man though.
Bravely and patiently he still pursued
The difference between the soul and matter.
He never found it but that 'Cogito'
Stressed, he made clear, 'I know myself,
No other'. And so tonight I think
30 With admiration of this generous thinker,
This self-denying seeker as my mind
Swarms with what poetry is, why poems are made
And 'I write poems therefore I am' won't do

Nor, though perhaps it's closer, 'Poems write
Under the poet's partial power, therefore
They are.' The night is warm for mid-October,
The windows open and green smells come in,
A half-moon is engaged on staring at
This little planet. I yawn and I sense
40 That clarity which sometimes comes before
Sleep trespasses upon us, I feel (yes,
Not think) that poems or their substance are
Upheld by moon and stars, lifted by winds
But won't be words until some poet catches
The moment and the music. I'm still back
At a beginning I've known half my life.
So maybe poems sing out the greater questions
But questions which expect the answer yes.

The World We Made

We were aware of everything but ourselves,
    Listened, watched and thought
We did everything totally, never by halves,
    Intricate kingdoms were wrought

By the network and depth of our imagination.
    Everything that we saw
Or heard or touched or smelt was part of a passion
    And we were alert to awe.

One day we put a little cochineal
10   Into an eggcup and
From it made a world which was more real
    Than the one which was close at hand.

The god we worshipped we named Cochineal
    And he was a Sun God.
We shaped a totem pole and painted all
    The angriest things we could

Think of on it – red faces, skulls and knives
    And round it we danced, of course.
Upon such games as this a childhood thrives
20   And builds up such a force

Of memories, foretellings, wise delights.
    Everything had a place
In our dervish dances, our cardboard swords, our rites
    And all had an odd grace.

Maybe because order was everywhere
    Nothing was meaningless
But my father was troubled and one day said, 'You are
    Christians, you know.' His distress

Was something that we could not understand
30   Yet trespassing on our world
He had overshadowed and spoilt it for us and
    Our fervour soon grew cold.

Our Sun God stayed in the sky and somehow had
    Lost most of its power.
Of course we were grateful for it when it shed
    Its heat upon us but our

Religion had foundered on what we did not know
    Was called reality then.
We forgot our dances and rites and started to grow
40   Like the dullard rest of men.

The world outside us hadn't changed but we
    Found imagination was
Something to do with art and poetry.
    Our great world came to a close.

Cochineal was drawn back to a bottle
    Of colouring essence, our pole
Was lost in an attic while we ourselves had to settle
    Down in a world not whole

Or satisfying or orderly while we
50   Shrank into teenagers who,
Conscious of little but themselves, aren't free
    To dream but must learn to know.

It Is Not True?

It comes to me at midnight it is true
We don't believe in death. It can't be so
Or not for those we know as me and you.

It is a state, a happening, an event
For those who're strangers to us. Death is meant
For others. In newspapers in dark print

We read of great ones going. We think of
The fact a moment, then turn back to love
And care and all the ways that we must move

10 To work, to play, while death goes on elsewhere.
It is a message carried through the air,
Something that happened when we were not there.

But wait, a day arrives when someone close
Is taken ill and dies. We feel the loss
And thoughts of our own deaths return to us.

My mother died two years ago today.
I often think of questions I could say
That only she could answer. She's away

But where and how? O love, we quarrel and
20 Neither will speak. Then one puts out a hand
The other takes. We start to understand

Our final goings and we are afraid
And I, not you, believe we are not made
To go forever. When we often said

Death is not true, I think we were in part
Precisely right. When we make works of art
We think they'll last. O when did mankind start

To think of death as somehow to begin
Our lives a different way, to start again
30   And live life flawlessly? Our minds move in

Countries untried but waiting for us. Love
Conjures up lands which death knows nothing of
And forevers are convincing proof,

And hint at lastings. Love goes further still,
Suggesting we have spirits death can't kill.
O love I am afraid of this as well.

Still Life

but it isn't
the painter is playing
a very beautiful (usually)
trick. Think of Cézanne's *Apples*
or a narrow vase of flowers by Chardin
or a pair of old boots
by Van Gogh
who could also make you care for
a chair or a bed
10 long before Pop artists
or Op ones thought they were making
you look at a chair closely
simply by putting a solid one
on a very small platform
I won't say a 'real' one
because art is all an illusion
but a mysterious one that somehow
takes you to truth by imitation
because Cézanne's *apples*
20 and Van Gogh's *chair*
look utterly unlike
anything you have eaten
or sat on, and Chardin's vase of flowers
is his own, in his style
and that is important.
Style is the great illusion in art
and only man notices it
or uses it.
Still Lives
30 are moving us almost to tears,
to amazement.

Introduction by Carol Ann Duffy

Like many children, reading stories and poems at school and at home was something I loved. As I grew, and became an older child and then an adolescent, I began more and more to write poems myself. I would say now that I began to be aware of a vocation – that I wanted the reading and writing of poetry to be an important part of my life. Although at first I vaguely thought that all poets were Dead Men, the growing popularity of poetry readings (in the early 1970s), the availability of new poetry collections (notably The Penguin Modern Poets series), and the influence in many areas, including literature, of the Women's Movement all helped my confidence and development as a young female writer.

Some of the poems in this selection are among the earliest I published and are autobiographical, drawing directly on my own Catholic background (*Ash Wednesday 1984* [p.90]; *Words of Absolution* [p.91]). Some are poems about, or in the voices of people I know in my private life or have encountered in my working life. *Head of English* (p.85) is a true story, rendered as a monologue. *Recognition* (p.88), another female voice, is a fictionalized account of a real menopause. Some poems have been prompted by paintings – *Standing Female Nude* (p.86) by a painting by Georges Braque; *The Virgin Punishing the Infant* (p.94) by a painting by Max Ernst. But whatever the starting-point of the poem – a voice, an image, a memory, a dolphin, or a murder – the energy it required to be written at all, to render it as language, was my own attraction to it. A poet's attraction to their subject can be emotional or intellectual, sometimes both, and the language the poet tries to find for the poem can be simple or complex. In my own case, being drawn by both instinct and myopia to 'voice', I have tried to let the subjects of my poems, including me, speak for themselves.

Head of English

Today we have a poet in the class.
A real live poet with a published book.
Notice the inkstained fingers girls. Perhaps
we're going to witness verse hot from the press.
Who knows. Please show your appreciation
by clapping. Not too loud. Now

sit up straight and listen. Remember
the lesson on assonance, for not all poems,
sadly, rhyme these days. Still. Never mind.
10 Whispering's, as always, out of bounds—
but do feel free to raise some questions.
After all, we're paying forty pounds.

Those of you with English Second Language
see me after break. We're fortunate
to have this person in our midst.
Season of mists and so on and so forth.
I've written quite a bit of poetry myself,
am doing Kipling with the Lower Fourth.

Right. That's enough from me. On with the Muse.
20 Open a window at the back. We don't
want winds of change about the place.
Take notes, but don't write reams. Just an essay
on the poet's themes. Fine. Off we go.
Convince us that there's something we don't know.

Well. Really. Run along now girls. I'm sure
that gave an insight to an outside view.
Applause will do. Thank you
very much for coming here today. Lunch
in the hall? Do hang about. Unfortunately
30 I have to dash. Tracey will show you out.

Standing Female Nude

Six hours like this for a few francs.
Belly nipple arse in the window light,
he drains the colour from me. Further to the right,
Madame. And do try to be still.
I shall be represented analytically and hung
in great museums. The bourgeoisie will coo
at such an image of a river-whore. They call it Art.

Maybe. He is concerned with volume, space.
I with the next meal. You're getting thin,
10 Madame, this is not good. My breasts hang
slightly low, the studio is cold. In the tea-leaves
I can see the Queen of England gazing
on my shape. Magnificent, she murmurs
moving on. It makes me laugh. His name

is Georges. They tell me he's a genius.
There are times he does not concentrate
and stiffens for my warmth. Men think of their mothers.
He possesses me on canvas as he dips the brush
repeatedly into the paint. Little man,
20 you've not the money for the arts I sell.
Both poor, we make our living how we can.

I ask him Why do you do this? Because
I have to. There's no choice. Don't talk.
My smile confuses him. These artists
take themselves too seriously. At night I fill myself
with wine and dance around the bars. When it's finished
he shows me proudly, lights a cigarette. I say
Twelve francs and get my shawl. It does not look like me.

A Healthy Meal

The gourmet tastes the secret dreams of cows
tossed lightly in garlic. Behind the green door, swish
of oxtails languish on an earthen dish. Here are
wishbones and pinkies; fingerbowls will absolve guilt.

Capped teeth chatter to a kidney or at the breast
of something which once flew. These hearts knew
no love and on their beds of saffron rice they lie
beyond reproach. What is the claret like? Blood.

On table six, the language of tongues is braised
10   in armagnac. The woman chewing suckling pig
must sleep with her husband later. Leg,
saddle and breast bleat against pure white cloth.

Alter *calf* to *veal* in four attempts. This is
the power of words; knife, tripe, lights, charcuterie.
A fat man orders his *rare* and a fine sweat
bastes his face. There are napkins to wipe the evidence

and sauces to gag the groans of abattoirs. The menu
lists the recent dead in French, from which they order
offal, poultry, fish. Meat flops in the jowls. Belch.
20   Death moves in the bowels. You are what you eat.

Recognition

Things get away from one.
I've let myself go, I know.
Children? I've had three
and don't even know them.

I strain to remember a time
when my body felt lighter.
Years. My face is swollen
with regrets. I put powder on,

      but it flakes off. I love him,
10   through habit, but the proof
has evaporated. He gets upset.
I tried to do all the essentials

on one trip. Foolish, yes,
but I was weepy all morning.
Quiche. A blond boy swung me up
in his arms and promised the earth.

You see, this came back to me
as I stood on the scales.
I wept. Shallots. In the window,
20   creamy ladies held a pose

which left me clogged and old.
The waste. I'd forgotten my purse,
fumbled; the shopgirl gaped at me,
compassionless. Claret. I blushed.

Cheese. Kleenex. *It did happen.*
I lay in my slip on wet grass,
laughing. Years. I had to rush out,
blind in a hot flush, and bumped

into an anxious, dowdy matron
30   who touched the cold mirror
and stared at me. Stared
and said I'm sorry sorry sorry.

The Dolphins

World is what you swim in, or dance, it is simple.
We are in our element but we are not free.
Outside this world you cannot breathe for long.
The other has my shape. The other's movement
forms my thoughts. And also mine. There is a man
and there are hoops. There is a constant flowing guilt.

We have found no truth in these waters,
no explanations tremble on our flesh.
We were blessed and now we are not blessed.
10   After travelling such space for days we began
to translate. It was the same space. It is
the same space always and above it is the man.

And now we are no longer blessed, for the world
will not deepen to dream in. The other knows
and out of love reflects me for myself.
We see our silver skin flash by like memory
of somewhere else. There is a coloured ball
we have to balance till the man has disappeared.

The moon has disappeared. We circle well-worn grooves
20   of water on a single note. Music of loss forever
from the other's heart which turns my own to stone.
There is a plastic toy. There is no hope. We sink
to the limits of this pool until the whistle blows.
There is a man and our mind knows we will die here.

Ash Wednesday 1984

In St Austin's and Sacré Coeur the accents of ignorance
sing out. The Catholic's spanking wains are marked
by a bigot's thumbprint dipped in burnt black palm.
Dead language rises up and does them harm.

I remember this. The giving up of gobstoppers
for Lent, the weekly invention of venial sin
in a dusty box. Once, in pale blue dresses,
we kissed petals for the Bishop's feet.

Stafford's guilty sinners slobbered at their beads, beneath
10   the purple-shrouded plaster saints. We were Scottish,
moved down there for work, and every Sunday
I was leathered up the road to Church.

Get to Communion and none of your cheek.
We'll put the fear of God in your bones.
Swallow the Eucharist, humble and meek.
St Stephen was martyred with stones.

It makes me sick. My soul is not a vest
spattered with wee black marks. Miracles and shamrocks
and transubstantiation are all my ass.
20   For Christ's sake, do not send your kids to Mass.

Words of Absolution

She clings to life by a rosary,
ninety years old. Who made you?
God made me. Pearl died a bairn
and him blacklisted. Listen
to the patterns of your prayers
down the years. What is Purgatory?

The guilt and stain of Original Sin.
Except the Virgin. Never a drink
or tobacco and the legs opened only
10   for childbirth. Forgive me. With her
they pass the parcel. Don't let the music
stop and me holding it. What do you mean
by the resurrection of the body?

Blessed art thou among women even if
we put you in a home. Only the silent motion
of lips and the fingering of decades.
How do we show that we love God?
Never a slack shilling, but good broth
always on the table. Which are the fasting days?
20   Mary Wallace, what are the days of abstinence?

Chrism, ash, holy water, beads
waiting for the end of nothing. Granny,
I have committed the Sin of Sodom.
How are we to love one another?
What are the four last things
to be ever remembered? I go to my reward.
Chastity. Piety. Modesty. Longanimity.
How should you finish the day? After
your night prayers what should you do?

Psychopath

I run my metal comb through the D.A. and pose
my reflection between dummies in the window at Burton's.
Lamp light. Jimmy Dean. All over town, ducking and
    diving,
my shoes scud sparks against the night. She is in the canal.
Let me make myself crystal. With a good-looking girl
    crackling
in four petticoats, you feel like a king. She rode past me
on a wooden horse, laughing, and the air sang *Johnny,
Remember Me*. I turned the world faster, flash.

I don't talk much. I swing up beside them and do it
10 with my eyes. Brando. She was clean. I could smell her.
I thought, Here we go, old son. The fairground spun
    round us
and she blushed like candyfloss. You can woo them
with goldfish and coconuts, whispers in the Tunnel of Love.
When I zip up the leather, I'm in a new skin, I touch it
and love myself, sighing Some little lady's going to get lucky
tonight. My breath wipes me from the looking-glass.

We move from place to place. We leave on the last
    morning
with the scent of local girls on our fingers. They wear
our lovebites on their necks. I know what women want,
20 a handrail to Venus. She said *Please* and *Thank you*
to the toffee-apple, teddy-bear. I thought I was on, no
    error.
She squealed on the dodgems, clinging to my leather sleeve.
I took a swig of whisky from the flask and frenched it
down her throat. *No*, she said, *Don't*, like they always do.

Dirty Alice flicked my dick out when I was twelve.
She jeered. I nicked a quid and took her to the spinney.
I remember the wasps, the sun blazing as I pulled
her knickers down. I touched her and I went hard,
but she grabbed my hand and used that, moaning . . .
30 She told me her name on the towpath, holding the fish
in a small sack of water. We walked away from the lights.
She'd come too far with me now. She looked back, once.

A town like this would kill me. A gypsy read my palm.
She saw fame. I could be anything with my looks,
my luck, my brains. I bought a guitar and blew a smoke
      ring
at the moon. Elvis nothing. *I'm not that type*, she said.
Too late. I eased her down by the dull canal
and talked sexy. Useless. She stared at the goldfish, silent.
I grabbed the plastic bag. She cried as it gasped and
      wriggled
40 on the grass and here we are. A dog craps by a lamp post.

Mama, straight up, I hope you rot in hell. The old man
sloped off, sharpish. I saw her through the kitchen window.
The sky slammed down on my school cap, chicken licken.
Lady, Sweetheart, Princess I say now, but I never stay.
My sandwiches were near her thigh, then the Rent Man
lit her cigarette and I ran, ran . . . She is in the canal.
These streets are quiet, as if the town has held its breath
to watch the Wheel go round above the dreary homes.

No, don't. Imagine. One thump did it, then I was on her,
50 giving her everything I had. Jack the Lad, Ladies' Man.
Easier to say Yes. Easier to stay a child, wide-eyed
at the top of the helter-skelter. You get one chance in
      this life
and if you screw it you're done for, uncle, no mistake.

She lost a tooth. I picked her up, dead slim, and slid her in.
A girl like that should have a paid-up solitaire and high
    hopes,
but she asked for it. A right-well knackered outragement.

My reflection sucks a sour Woodbine and buys me a drink.
    Here's
looking at you. Deep down I'm talented. She found out.
    Don't mess
with me, angel, I'm no nutter. Over in the corner, a dead
    ringer
60   for Ruth Ellis smears a farewell kiss on the lip of a gin-and-
    lime.
The barman calls Time. Bang in the centre of my skull,
there's a strange coolness. I could almost fly. Tomorrow
will find me elsewhere, with a loss of memory. Drink
    up son,
the world's your fucking oyster. Awopbopaloobop
    alopbimbam.

The Virgin Punishing the Infant
After the painting by Max Ernst

He spoke early. Not the *goo goo goo* of infancy,
but *I am God.* Joseph kept away, carving himself
a silent Pinocchio out in the workshed. He said
he was a simple man and hadn't dreamed of this.

She grew anxious in that second year, would stare
at stars saying *Gabriel? Gabriel?* Your guess.
The village gossiped in the sun. The child was solitary,
his wide and solemn eyes could fill your head.

After he walked, our normal children crawled. Our wives
10 were first resentful, then superior. Mary's child
would bring her sorrow . . . better far to have a son
who gurgled nonsense at your breast. *Googoo. Googoo.*

But I am God. We heard him through the window,
heard the smacks which made us peep. What we saw
was commonplace enough. But afterwards, we wondered
why the infant did not cry. And why the Mother did.

Foreign

Imagine living in a strange, dark city for twenty years.
There are some dismal dwellings on the east side
and one of them is yours. On the landing, you hear
your foreign accent echo down the stairs. You think
in a language of your own and talk in theirs.

Then you are writing home. The voice in your head
recites the letter in a local dialect; behind that
is the sound of your mother singing to you,
all that time ago, and now you do not know
10 why your eyes are watering and what's the word for this.

You use the public transport. Work. Sleep. Imagine one
    night
you saw a name for yourself sprayed in red
against a brick wall. A hate name. Red like blood.
It is snowing on the streets, under the neon lights,
as if this place were coming to bits before your eyes.

And in the delicatessen, from time to time, the coins
in your palm will not translate. Inarticulate,
because this is not home, you point at fruit. Imagine
that one of you says *Me not know what these people mean.*
20 *It like they only go to bed and dream.* Imagine that.

Making Money

Turnover. Profit. Readies. Cash. Loot. Dough. Income.
    Stash.
Dosh. Bread. Finance. Brass. I give my tongue over
to money; the taste of warm rust in a chipped mug
of tap-water. Drink some yourself. Consider
an Indian man in Delhi, Salaamat the *niyariwallah*,
who squats by an open drain for hours, sifting shit
for the price of a chapati. More than that. His hands
in crumbling gloves of crap pray at the drains
for the pearls in slime his grandfather swore he found.

10 Megabucks. Wages. Interest. Wealth. I sniff and snuffle
for a whiff of pelf; the stench of an abattoir blown
by a stale wind over the fields. Roll up a fiver,
snort. Meet Kim. Kim will give you the works,
her own worst enema, suck you, lick you, squeal
red weals to your whip, be nun, nurse, nanny,
nymph on a credit card. Don't worry.
Kim's only in it for the money. Lucre. Tin. Dibs.

I put my ear to brass lips; a small fire's whisper
close to a forest. Listen. His cellular telephone
20 rings in the Bull's car. Golden hello. Big deal. Now get this
straight. *Making a living is making a killing these days.*
Jobbers and brokers buzz. He paints out a landscape
by number. The Bull. Seriously rich. Nasty. One of us.

Salary. Boodle. Oof. Blunt. Shekels. Lolly. Gelt. Funds.
I wallow in coin, naked; the scary caress of a fake hand
on my flesh. Get stuck in. Bergama. The boys from the
    bazaar
hide on the target-range, watching the soldiers fire.
    Between bursts,
they rush for the spent shells, cart them away for scrap.
Here is the catch. Some shells don't explode. Ahmat
30 runs over grass, lucky for six months, so far. So
bomb-collectors die young. But the money's good.

Palmgrease. Smackers. Greenbacks. Wads. I widen my eyes
at a fortune; a set of knives on black cloth, shining,
utterly beautiful. Weep. The economy booms
like cannon, far out at sea on a lone ship. We leave
our places of work, tired, in the shortening hours, in the
    time
of night our town could be anywhere, and some of us pause
in the square, where a clown makes money swallowing fire.

Letters from Deadmen

Beneath the earth a perfect femur glows. I recall
a little pain and then a century of dust. Observe my
    anniversary,
place purple violets tenderly before the urn. You must.
No one can hear the mulching of the heart, which
    thrummed
with blood or drummed with love. Perhaps, by now,
your sadness will be less. Unless you still remember me.

I flung silver pigeons to grey air with secret messages
for men I had not met. Do they ever mention me
at work and was there weeping in the crematorium?
10 Dear wife, dear child, I hope you leave my room
exactly as it was. The pipe, the wireless and, of course,
the cricket photographs. They say we rest in peace.

Ash or loam. Scattered or slowly nagged by worms. I lie
above my parents in the family plot and I fit neatly
in a metal cask in ever-loving memory of myself.
They parted his garments, casting lots upon them
what every man should take. A crate of stout.
Small talk above the salmon sandwiches. Insurance men.

But here you cannot think. The voice-box imitates
20 the skeletons of leaves. Words snail imperceptibly and
    soundless
in the soil. Dear love, remember me. Give me biography
beyond these simple dates. Were there psalms and hired
    limousines?
All this eternally before my final breath and may
this find you as it leaves me here. Eventually.

Small Female Skull

With some surprise, I balance my small female skull in
      my hands.
What is it like? An ocarina? Blow in its eye.
It cannot cry, holds my breath only as long as I exhale,
mildly alarmed now, into the hole where the nose was,
press my ear to its grin. A vanishing sigh.

For some time, I sit on the lavatory seat with my head
in my hands, appalled. It feels much lighter than I'd
      thought;
the weight of a deck of cards, a slim volume of verse,
but with something else, as though it could levitate.
      Disturbing.
10 So why do I kiss it on the brow, my warm lips to its
      papery bone,

and take it to the mirror to ask for a gottle of geer?
I rinse it under the tap, watch dust run away, like sand
from a swimming-cap, then dry it – firstborn – gently
with a towel. I see the scar where I fell for sheer love
down treacherous stairs, and read that shattering day
      like braille.

Love, I murmur to my skull, then, louder, other
      grand words,
shouting the hollow nouns in a white-tiled room.
Downstairs they will think I have lost my mind. No. I
      only weep
into these two holes here, or I'm grinning back at the
      joke, this is
20 a friend of mine. See, I hold her face in trembling,
      passionate hands.

The Grammar of Light

Even barely enough light to find a mouth,
and bless both with a meaningless O, teaches,
spells out. The way a curtain opened at night
lets in neon, or moon, or a car's hasty glance,
and paints for a moment someone you love, pierces.

And so many mornings to learn; some
when the day is wrung from damp, grey skies
and rooms come on for breakfast
in the town you are leaving early. The way
10 a wasteground weeps glass tears at the end of a street.

Some fluent, showing you how the trees
in the square think in birds, telepathize. The way
the waiter balances light in his hands, the coins
in his pocket silver, and a young bell shines
in its white tower ready to tell.

Even a saucer of rain in a garden at evening
speaks to the eye. Like the little fires
from allotments, undressing in veils of mauve smoke
as you walk home under the muted lamps,
20 perplexed. The way the shy stars go stuttering on.

And at midnight, a candle next to the wine
slurs its soft wax, flatters. Shadows
circle the table. The way all faces blur
to dreams of themselves held in the eyes.
The flare of another match. The way everything dies.

Prayer

Some days, although we cannot pray, a prayer
utters itself. So, a woman will lift
her head from the sieve of her hands and stare
at the minims sung by a tree, a sudden gift.

Some nights, although we are faithless, the truth
enters our hearts, that small familiar pain;
then a man will stand stock-still, hearing his youth
in the distant Latin chanting of a train.

Pray for us now. Grade I piano scales
10   console the lodger looking out across
a Midlands town. Then dusk, and someone calls
a child's name as though they named their loss.

Darkness outside. Inside, the radio's prayer—
Rockall. Malin. Dogger. Finisterre.

Introduction by Eavan Boland

When I was a student at Trinity I went to Achill Island, off the coast of Mayo for a few days. It was Easter time and by day there was a brilliant aspect to the island. The air was less humid than on the east coast. All the blues and greens were harsh and clear. But by evening a bitter wind came in from the Atlantic and you had to go indoors and start a fire with turf blocks to keep even passably warm. There was no water in the cottage and just before dusk an old woman would bring some and leave it with me. Afterwards, we stood talking in the last, icy light. She pointed out the cliffs over the ocean and the remains of a village and told me something of the 1847 famine, when the potato crop had failed, causing widespread devastation in those parts. She showed me the slope of the cliff down which the villagers had moved so as to be closer to the seaweed on the shore, which was all they had to eat.

The cold light, the dignity of her talk, the contrast with my own uncertainty about history and knowledge, all stayed with me. *The Achill Woman* (p.109) revisits the occasion. I had come to Achill as a student, carrying a book of British court poetry, a set text for the spring exams in Trinity that year. I went ready to memorize the odes and elegies from another country: some of them powerful codes of loss and power. And then with scalding irony, a woman seemed to speak from the most silent sources of dispossession and memory. I felt, rightly or wrongly, that I had heard a voice speaking from outside history. And I should follow.

Many of the poems in this selection are part of that following. 'Poetry' said Rilke 'is the past that breaks out in our hearts'. But who has the right to describe that past? Who is authorized to tell that story? In trying to think about those questions I began to see that my life was lived in their shadow. When I left Trinity, I married, went to live in Dundrum, a suburb outside Dublin, and had two children. One summer evening in the suburb, with the fuschia darkening, and the light going from behind the hills, it seemed to me crucial that I should be able to put the life I lived into the poems I wrote. And yet the poems I learned to write as a young poet, and the literary culture around them, seemed to have no name for that life. I had to name it myself. A poem like *Suburban Woman: a Detail* (p.106) is an exact narrative of my sense of the life around me in a place which was not marked on the poetic map, but was full of lyric power, just as *Lace* (p.108) is an account of trying to record it.

Maps. The official version. The making of history. Several poems here try to question those processes. *That the Science of Cartography is Limited* (p.117), for instance, is about the famine roads which the victims of the 1847 famine were given to build by the Relief Committees, and which they had no strength to complete. Those roads are the scar tissue of Irish history. They wander off into darkness in countless woods and beside innumerable verges. Where they stop is where the makers died. And yet they appear on no map of Ireland that I have ever seen. A different argument, but the same theme, occurs in *The Dolls' Museum in Dublin* (p.118). The dolls' museum is not far from my house. I went in there with my thirteen-year-old daughter one Sunday. Most of them were Irish dolls, probably Edwardian, dressed in worn lace and thinned-out silk. Their eyes were china blue and stared straight ahead. It was impossible not to think of what witnesses they must have been to the events of Irish history. And I imagine them as part of the decorum that is swept away by violence.

In my generation, Irish women have gone from being the objects of the Irish poem to being its authors. It has been a powerful and disruptive change. Not surprisingly perhaps, the process of naming, of speaking, of breaking a silence is in several of these poems, including *Anna Liffey* (p.122). The doorway of our house faces south-east to the Dublin hills, behind which are the Wicklow mountains. Between them, in a place called The Sally Gap, the River Liffey rises as a small, inconsequential trickle and flows under thirteen bridges to the sea. The poem, at least in part, is about how the landscape and femininity are often confused, and how that confusion depends on the silence of both. And how, once that silence is broken, a different story emerges.

The Woman Changes her Skin

How often
in this loneliness,
unlighted
but for the porcelain

brightening
of the bath,
have I done this.
Again and again this.

This time,
10 in the shadowy
and woody light
between the bath and blind,

between the day and night,
the same blue
eyeshadow,
rouge and blusher,

will mesh
with my fingers
to a weaving
20 pulse.

In a ringed
coiling,
a convulsion,
I will heave

to a sinuous
and final
shining off
of skin:

look at the hood
30   I have made
for my eyes,
my head

and how quickly
over my lips,
slicked and cold,
my tongue flickers.

Suburban Woman: a Detail

I

The chimneys have been swept.
The gardens have their winter cut.
The shrubs are prinked, the hedges gelded.

The last dark shows up the headlights
of the cars coming down the Dublin mountains.

Our children used to think they were stars.

II

This is not the season
when the goddess rose
out of seed, out of wheat,
10   out of thawed water
and went, distracted and astray,
to find her daughter.

Winter will be soon:
Dun pools of rain;
ruddy, addled distances;
winter pinks, tinges and
a first-thing smell of turf
when I take the milk in.

III

Setting out for a neighbour's house
20   in a denim skirt,

a blouse blended in
by the last light,

I am definite
to start with
but the light is lessening,
the hedge losing its detail,
the path its edge.

Look at me, says the tree.
I was a woman once like you,
30   full-skirted, human.

Suddenly I am not certain
of the way I came
or the way I will return,
only that something
which may be nothing
more than darkness has begun
softening the definitions
of my body, leaving

the fears and all the terrors
40   of the flesh shifting the airs
and forms of the autumn quiet

crying 'remember us'.

Lace

Bent over
the open notebook—

light fades out
making the trees stand out
and my room
at the back
of the house, dark.

In the dusk
I am still
10   looking for it—
the language that is

lace:

a baroque obligation
at the wrist
of a prince
in a petty court.
Look, just look
at the way he shakes out

the thriftless phrases,
20   the crystal rhetoric
of bobbined knots
and bosses:
a vagrant drift
of emphasis
to wave away an argument
or frame the hand
he kisses;
which, for all that, is still

what someone
30 in the corner
of a room,
in the dusk,
bent over
as the light was fading

lost their sight for.

The Achill Woman

She came up the hill carrying water.
She wore a half-buttoned, wool cardigan,
a tea-towel round her waist.

She pushed the hair out of her eyes with
her free hand and put the bucket down.

The zinc-music of the handle on the rim
tuned the evening. An Easter moon rose.
In the next-door field a stream was
a fluid sunset; and then, stars.

10 I remember the cold rosiness of her hands.
She bent down and blew on them like broth.
And round her waist, on a white background,
in coarse, woven letters, the words 'glass cloth'.

And she was nearly finished for the day.
And I was all talk, raw from college—
week-ending at a friend's cottage
with one suitcase and the set text
of the Court poets of the Silver Age.

We stayed putting down time until
20   the evening turned cold without warning.
She said goodnight and started down the hill.

The grass changed from lavender to black.
The trees turned back to cold outlines.
You could taste frost

but nothing now can change the way I went
indoors, chilled by the wind
and made a fire
and took down my book
and opened it and failed to comprehend

30   the harmonies of servitude,
the grace music gives to flattery
and language borrows from ambition—

and how I fell asleep
oblivious to

the planets clouding over in the skies,
the slow decline of the Spring moon,
the songs crying out their ironies.

The Making of an Irish Goddess

Ceres went to hell
with no sense of time.

When she looked back
all that she could see was

the arteries of silver in the rock,
the diligence of rivers always at one level,
wheat at one height,
leaves of a single colour,
the same distance in the usual light;

10 a seasonless, unscarred earth.

But I need time—
my flesh and that history—
to make the same descent.

In my body,
neither young now nor fertile,
and with the marks of childbirth
still on it,

in my gestures—
the way I pin my hair to hide
20 the stitched, healed blemish of a scar—
must be

an accurate inscription
of that agony:

the failed harvests,
the fields rotting to the horizon,
the children devoured by their mothers
whose souls, they would have said,
went straight to hell,
followed by their own.

30 There is no other way:

myth is the wound we leave
in the time we have—

which in my case is this
March evening
at the foothills of the Dublin mountains,
across which the lights have changed all day,

holding up my hand
sickle-shaped, to my eyes
to pick out
40 my own daughter from
all the other children in the distance;

her back turned to me.

Outside History

There are outsiders, always. These stars—
these iron inklings of an Irish January,
whose light happened

thousands of years before
our pain did: they are, they have always been
outside history.

They keep their distance. Under them remains
a place where you found
you were human, and

10 a landscape in which you know you are mortal.
And a time to choose between them.
I have chosen:

out of myth into history I move to be
part of that ordeal
whose darkness is

only now reaching me from those fields,
those rivers, those roads clotted as
firmaments with the dead.

How slowly they die
20 as we kneel beside them, whisper in their ear.
And we are too late. We are always too late.

The Pomegranate

The only legend I have ever loved is
the story of a daughter lost in hell.
And found and rescued there.
Love and blackmail are the gist of it.
Ceres and Persephone the names.
And the best thing about the legend is
I can enter it anywhere. And have.
As a child in exile in
a city of fogs and strange consonants,
10   I read it first and at first I was
an exiled child in the crackling dusk of
the underworld, the stars blighted. Later
I walked out in a summer twilight
searching for my daughter at bed-time.
When she came running I was ready
to make any bargain to keep her.
I carried her back past whitebeams
and wasps and honey-scented buddleias.
But I was Ceres then and I knew
20   winter was in store for every leaf
on every tree on that road.
Was inescapable for each one we passed.
And for me.
                    It is winter
and the stars are hidden.
I climb the stairs and stand where I can see
my child asleep beside her teen magazines,
her can of Coke, her plate of uncut fruit.
The pomegranate! How did I forget it?
30   She could have come home and been safe
and ended the story and all
our heart-broken searching but she reached
out a hand and plucked a pomegranate.

She put out her hand and pulled down
the French sound for apple and
the noise of stone and the proof
that even in the place of death,
at the heart of legend, in the midst
of rocks full of unshed tears
40 ready to be diamonds by the time
the story was told, a child can be
hungry. I could warn her. There is still a chance.
The rain is cold. The road is flint-coloured.
The suburb has cars and cable television.
The veiled stars are above ground.
It is another world. But what else
can a mother give her daughter but such
beautiful rifts in time?
If I defer the grief I will diminish the gift.
50 The legend will be hers as well as mine.
She will enter it. As I have.
She will wake up. She will hold
the papery flushed skin in her hand.
And to her lips. I will say nothing.

The Parcel

There are dying arts and
one of them is
the way my mother used to make up a parcel.
Paper first. Mid-brown and coarse-grained as wood.
The worst sort for covering a Latin book neatly
or laying flat at Christmas on a pudding bowl.
It was a big cylinder. She snipped it open
and it unrolled quickly across the floor.
All business, all distance.

10   Then the scissors.
Not a glittering let-up but a dour
pair, black thumb-holes,
the shears themselves the colour of the rained-
on steps a man with a grindstone climbed up
in the season of lilac and snapdragon
and stood there arguing the rate for
sharpening the lawnmower and the garden pair
and this one. All-in.
The ball of twine was coarsely braided

20   and only a shade less yellow than
the flame she held under the blunt
end of the sealing-wax until
it melted and spread into a brittle
terracotta medal.
Her hair dishevelled, her tongue between her teeth,
she wrote the address in the quarters
twine had divided the surface into.
Names and places. Crayon and fountain-pen.
The town underlined once. The country twice.

30   It's ready for the post
she would say and if we want to know
where it went to—
a craft lost before we missed it – watch it go
into the burlap sack for collection.
See it disappear. Say
this is how it died
out: among doomed steamships and out-dated trains,
the tracks for them disappearing before our eyes,
next to station names we can't remember

40   on a continent we no longer
recognize. The sealing-wax cracking.
The twine unravelling. The destination illegible.

That the Science of Cartography is Limited

– and not simply by the fact that this shading of
forest cannot show the fragrance of balsam,
the gloom of cypresses
is what I wish to prove.

When you and I were first in love we drove
to the borders of Connacht
and entered a wood there.

Look down you said: this was once a famine road.

I looked down at ivy and the scutch grass
10   rough-cast stone had
disappeared into as you told me
in the second winter of their ordeal, in

1847, when the crop had failed twice,
Relief Committees gave
the starving Irish such roads to build.

Where they died, there the road ended

and ends still and when I take down
the map of this island, it is never so
I can say here is
20   the masterful, the apt rendering of

the spherical as flat, nor
an ingenious design which persuades a curve
into a plane,
but to tell myself again that

the line which says woodland and cries hunger
and gives out among sweet pine and cypress,
and finds no horizon

will not be there.

The Dolls' Museum in Dublin

The wounds are terrible. The paint is old.
The cracks along the lips and on the cheeks
cannot be fixed. The cotton lawn is soiled.
The arms are ivory dissolved to wax.

Recall the Quadrille. Hum the waltz.
Promenade on the yacht-club terraces.
Put back the lamps in their copper holders,
the carriage wheels on the cobbled quays.

And recreate Easter in Dublin.
10   Booted officers. Their mistresses.
Sunlight criss-crossing College Green.
Steam hissing from the flanks of horses.

Here they are. Cradled and cleaned,
held close in the arms of their owners.
Their cold hands clasped by warm hands,
their faces memorized like perfect manners.

The altars are mannerly with linen.
The lilies are whiter than surplices.
The candles are burning and warning:
20 Rejoice, they whisper. After sacrifice.

Horse-chestnuts hold up their candles.
The Green is vivid with parasols.
Sunlight is pastel and windless.
The bar of the Shelbourne is full.

Laughter and gossip on the terraces.
Rumour and alarm at the barracks.
The Empire is summoning its officers.
The carriages are turning: they are turning back.

Past children walking with governesses,
30 Looking down, cossetting their dolls,
then looking up as the carriage passes,
the shadow chilling them. Twilight falls.

It is twilight in the dolls' museum. Shadows
remain on the parchment-coloured waists,
are bruises on the stitched cotton clothes,
are hidden in the dimples on the wrists.

The eyes are wide. They cannot address
the helplessness which has lingered in
the airless peace of each glass case:
40 to have survived. To have been stronger than

a moment. To be the hostages ignorance
takes from time and ornament from destiny. Both.
To be the present of the past. To infer the difference
with a terrible stare. But not feel it. And not know it.

Inscriptions

About holiday rooms there can be
a solid feel at first. Then, as you go upstairs,
the air gets
a dry rustle of excitement

the way a new dress comes out of tissue paper,
up and out of it, and
the girl watching this thinks:
Where will I wear it? Who will kiss me in it?

Peter
10   was the name on the cot.
The cot was made of the carefully-bought
scarcities of the nineteen-forties:
oak. Tersely planed and varnished.
Cast-steel hinges.

I stood where the roof sloped into
paper roses,
in a room where a child once went to sleep,
looking at blue, painted lettering:

as he slept
20   someone had found for him
five pieces of the alphabet which said
the mauve petals of his eyelids as they closed out
the scalded hallway moonlight made of the ocean at
the end of his road.

Someone knew
the importance of giving him a name.

For years I have known
how important it is
not to name
30   the coffins, the murdered in them,
the deaths in alleyways and on doorsteps—

in case they rise out of their names
and I recognize

the child who slept peacefully
and the girl who guessed at her future in
the dress as it came out of its box
falling free in
kick pleats of silk.

And what comfort can there be
40   in knowing that
in a distant room
his sign is safe tonight
and reposes its modest blues in darkness?

Or that outside his window
the name-eating elements – the salt wind, the rain—
must find
headstones to feed their hunger?

Anna Liffey

Life, the story goes,
Was the daughter of Cannan,
And came to the plain of Kildare.
She loved the flat-lands and the ditches
And the unreachable horizon.
She asked that it be named for her.
The river took its name from the land.
The land took its name from a woman.

A woman in the doorway of a house.
10 A river in the city of her birth.

There, in the hills above my house,
The river Liffey rises, is a source.
It rises in rush and ling heather and
Black peat and bracken and strengthens
To claim the city it narrated.
Swans. Steep falls. Small towns.
The smudged air and bridges of Dublin.

Dusk is coming.
Rain is moving east from the hills.

20 If I could see myself
I would see
A woman in a doorway
Wearing the colours that go with red hair.
Although my hair is no longer red.

I praise
The gifts of the river.
Its shiftless and glittering
Re-telling of a city,
Its clarity as it flows,
30 In the company of runt flowers and herons,
Around a bend at Islandbridge
And under thirteen bridges to the sea.
Its patience at twilight—
Swans nesting by it,
Neon wincing into it.

Maker of
Places, remembrances,
Narrate such fragments for me:

One body. One spirit.
40 One place. One name.
The city where I was born.
The river that runs through it.
The nation which eludes me

Fractions of a life
It has taken me a lifetime
To claim.

I came here in a cold winter.

I had no children. No country.
I did not know the name for my own life.

50 My country took hold of me.
My children were born.

I walked out in a summer dusk
To call them in.

One name. Then the other one.
The beautiful vowels sounding out home.

Make of a nation what you will
Make of the past
What you can—

There is now
60   A woman in a doorway.

It has taken me
All my strength to do this.

Becoming a figure in a poem.

Usurping a name and a theme.

A river is not a woman.
    Although the names it finds,
        The history it makes
And suffers—
        The Viking blades beside it,
70   The muskets of the Redcoats,
                The flames of the Four Courts
Blazing into it
    Are a sign.
        Any more than
A woman is a river,
    Although the course it takes,

Through swans courting and distraught willows,
Its patience
Which is also its powerlessness,
80   From Callary to Islandbridge,
   And from source to mouth,
Is another one.
    And in my late forties
Past believing
 Love will heal
  What language fails to know
And needs to say—
 What the body means—
  I take this sign
90 And I make this mark:
  A woman in the doorway of her house.
  A river in the city of her birth.
The truth of a suffered life.
  The mouth of it.

The seabirds come in from the coast.
The city wisdom is they bring rain.
I watch them from my doorway.
I see them as arguments of origin—
Leaving a harsh force on the horizon
100 Only to find it
Slanting and falling elsewhere.

Which water—
The one they leave or the one they pronounce—
Remembers the other?

I am sure
The body of an ageing woman
Is a memory

And to find a language for it
Is as hard
110 As weeping and requiring
These birds to cry out as if they could
Recognize their element
Remembered and diminished in
A single tear.

An ageing woman
Finds no shelter in language.
She finds instead
Single words she once loved
Such as 'summer' and 'yellow'
120 And 'sexual' and 'ready'
Have suddenly become dwellings
For someone else—
Rooms and a roof under which someone else
Is welcome, not her. Tell me,
Anna Liffey,
Spirit of water,
Spirit of place,
How is it on this
Rainy Autumn night
130 As the Irish sea takes
The names you made, the names
You bestowed, and gives you back
Only wordlessness?

Autumn rain is
Scattering and dripping
From car-ports
And clipped hedges.
The gutters are full.

When I came here
140 I had neither
Children nor country.
The trees were arms.
The hills were dreams.

I was free
To imagine a spirit
In the blues and greens,
The hills and fogs
Of a small city.

My children were born.
150 My country took hold of me.
A vision in a brick house.
Is it only love
That makes a place?

I feel it change.
My children are
Growing up, getting older.
My country holds on
To its own pain.

I turn off
160 The harsh yellow
Porch light and
Stand in the hall.
Where is home now?

Follow the rain
Out to the Dublin hills.
Let it become the river.
Let the spirit of place be
A lost soul again.

In the end
170 It will not matter
That I was a woman. I am sure of it.
The body is a source. Nothing more.
There is a time for it. There is a certainty
About the way it seeks its own dissolution.
Consider rivers.
They are always en route to
Their own nothingness. From the first moment
They are going home. And so
When language cannot do it for us,
180 Cannot make us know love will not diminish us,
There are these phrases
Of the ocean
To console us.
Particular and unafraid of their completion.
In the end
Everything that burdened and distinguished me
Will be lost in this:
I was a voice.

Notes

Poems by Emily Brontë

'High waving heather 'neath stormy blasts bending'

This poem is one of Emily Brontë's earliest and records a happiness rarely seen after 1838. Unlike later poems there is a more precise sense of a Yorkshire topography, running brooks, wild forests, heathery moors and the heavens thick with stars. Yet the scenery also has a traditionally Romantic colouring; it is a psychic landscape as well as a physical one.

You may notice here the poet's skilful use of rhythm and alliteration. Each line has four feet in a series of trochees. The fourth line of each stanza does not echo the second as we expect but is extended to mirror the first line thus producing a sense of energy and forward propulsion. The sixth line echoes the second and arrests this movement in a temporary calm but the whole poem has a feeling of a descending rapid, collecting at each level into a pool before plunging downwards again. Brontë may have been influenced by a reading of Robert Southey's poem *The Cataract of Lodore*.

Brontë was being taught painting and drawing by her sister Charlotte at this time. What kind of landscape does she depict? Note that earth and heaven seem to interconnect rather like in a Van Gogh painting. Technically, how does the poet create this impressionist style, this unstable yet dynamic mood? Notice her persistent use of a series of verbs in the continuous present tense. Which particular verbs describe violent forces? Why does the poem have no final focus?

1   This is an unusual beginning as it abandons any formal introduction of the subject. Note how the poet places the verb at the end of the line. This is a frequent device of Brontë's. The following are a few of her dramatic opening statements in the collection: *There let thy bleeding branch atone* (p.10); *Death that struck when I was most confiding* (p.15); *And first an hour of*

129

mournful musing (p.4). What effect does this odd syntax have?

6   **fetters**   chains designed to restrict the movement of the feet.

8   **life giving wind**   the image of wind as a restorative of the spirit is an important theme in Brontë's great novel *Wuthering Heights*. The heroine Catherine Earnshaw, sick with fever, throws open the window of her bedroom at Thrushcross Grange in order to breath the cold moorland air. In her delirium she sees Wuthering Heights, her old home, but fears that she can only reach it through death. You will notice as you read further that the image of wind develops and becomes part of Brontë's mystical vocabulary. See *The Night-Wind* (p.9), *A Farewell to Alexandria* (p.6), and particularly *The Prisoner* (p.19).

9   **jubilee**   an anniversary or celebration.

13   **lowering**   this may mean louring, threatening or angry.

'And first an hour of mournful musing'

This poem is interesting as an early attempt to describe the onset of mystical experience. Here, what was to become a familiar pattern of thought and feeling is established. Line 1 shows melancholy reflection, line 2, distress, lines 3-4, enforced calmness, line 5, a sudden lifting of the spirits, line 6, an intimation of spiritual contact and lines 7-8, a rapturous beholding. (See Notes to *The Prisoner*, p.141.)

At this stage in her poetry Brontë's mystical sense often seems frustrated by a cycle of intense but unstable emotions, resolved here by a somewhat vague idea of 'love'. In later poems she presents a more developed metaphysical structure – learned partly from Coleridge – but rooted in a deep personal belief in the spiritual world.

The poetic power of this early work is centred in its relentless rhythm punctuated by the repetition of *And* in the first three urgent lines of each stanza, followed by a calmer fourth line.

5   **throb**   does this imply the throbbing heart as well as the pulsing of *the glorious star* (8)?

8   **glorious star of love**   Venus.

'I'm happiest when most away'

Like the previous poem, this short, simple work describes a suspension of the self and a mystical oneness with the universe. It introduces again the theme of how the soul seems to stretch itself in contemplation of the night sky, what she was later to call the *space-sweeping soul* (*The Philosopher* [5]). See also the Notes to *Stars* (p.140).

There are three stages in Brontë's mysticism: one, pantheism or the worship of nature; two, stoicism – the development of an austere fortitude in the face of suffering; and three, quietism – a deliberate withdrawal of the will from all things of the senses. This poem belongs to the pantheistic mood in which the poet yearns for an 'out of the body' experience or a flight of the spirit which coincides with some mood in nature. This yearning to become a living soul may imply a death-wish and we shall see this idea in numerous later poems.

1   The first line is striking yet simple. The word *away* is left vague perhaps because the location of the soul on these flights is indefinable. This idea is echoed in the first line of the second stanza.

2   **home of clay**   a reference both to the grave and the physical body.

3   Note the sweeping rhythm here so characterisic of her poetry and its sense of elation.

8   **infinite immensity**   this Latinate phrase placed at the end of the poem suggests a vast, abstract concept contrasting with the more human but limited idea of 'happiness' mentioned in the first line. (See Approaches p.219 for a discussion of Brontë's idea of eternity.)

To the Blue Bell

This poem is characteristically Brontë with its suggested, but not defined, images of the Yorkshire moors. The sparseness of detail in her nature or landscape poetry – a single stone, flower or bird – creates a strange intimacy between the poet and object but she is interested less in particular features than universal forces. The *mountains wild* (4) and *deep green dells* (3) seem to be used here as an almost theatrical backdrop to the bluebell which she tenderly beholds less as a flower than as a *child* (2), a *darling* (8) and finally a *voice* (9).

9   In what way can a poet find a voice through something as small and delicate as a bluebell?

15-18   These are the words of the flower itself. How successful is this poetic device? What emotions are evoked and what is the bluebell's advice?

A Farewell to Alexandria

There is a long tradition of abandoned babes in literature and mythology. Sources may be found in classical Greek tragedy, Shakespeare (*The Winter's Tale*) and many fairy tales. You may wish to identify those features of the poem which recall familiar stories where childhood innocence is betrayed.

This poem is part of the Gondal series and records the abandonment of Alexandria, the dying infant daughter of Julius Brenzaida. The speaker is probably the child's mother Rosina of Alcona. It was first published under the title *The Outcast Mother* and has some similarities with Wordsworth's poem on a similar theme, *The Thorn*.

The poem begins with a reminiscence of a moorland dell bathed in the almost paradisal radiance of midsummer sun. It then moves to particular, consoling details of the *heather-bell* (5) nestling in some *storm-worn stone* (6) and the gently revitalizing wind, finally, returning in stanza six to the bleak reality of a winter landscape. Images of snow in Emily Brontë's poetry are almost obsessive. Snow is not merely a response to the harsh snow-bound winters at Haworth but is a symbol of innocence and purity overlaying the blackened images, the *tombstones grey* ('*I see around me tombstones grey*', p.11) of common reality. Remember that she rejected all notions of original sin – the Christian concept that man is born with a potential for evil.

5–6	Note the economical way in which the poet captures the loneliness of the landscape and the harshness of the weather.
7	Note the 'music' of the wind, a favourite metaphor.
12	**heath-sward** grass.
25–26	See Notes to line 7 of *Remembrance* (p.138).
35	**unblessed, unfriended child** unblessed by heaven or Christian burial.

'And now the house dog stretched once more'

This narrative fragment is interesting for its first description of the 'Heathcliff figure'. The setting is a homely shepherd's cottage. A picture of rustic happiness is drawn as the family basks in the warmth of a winter hearth. This relaxed, almost soporific mood is interrupted by the arrival of a stranger whose bowed figure and pallid brow are hidden beneath the folds of a cloak. The children at play remind us perhaps of Hindley and Catherine at the moment when Heathcliff arrives at Wuthering Heights, hidden under Mr Earnshaw's greatcoat. The stranger responds to the shepherd's spontaneous hospitality with chill abruptness. The sense of the destruction of a generous host hints at Mr Earnshaw's adoption of Heathcliff in *Wuthering Heights*.

1-2	**house dog** perhaps the poet's own mastiff, Keeper. Emily Brontë loved large, fierce dogs.
12	Required no special courtesy.
18	**froze** an acute contrast with the earlier image of fire. These stark opposites are common in the poems.
23-26	The stranger has a gipsy colouring, again reminiscent of Heathcliff?
30	**pride** the sin of Satan.
31-40	The look is of neither cruelty nor misery but of one who has gazed upon the supernatural.
40	**circling zone** the iris of the eye, here black.
46	**basilisk** a fabulous reptile also called a cockatrice because it was said to be hatched by a serpent from a cock's egg. Its look and breath were said to be fatal. The name, derived from the Greek word meaning 'royal', was so called from a spot resembling a crown or coronet on its head. The use of the word here may hint at fallen majesty.

The Night-Wind

Images of wind as spirit or as the breath of life were becoming central to the poet's thinking about the relationship of the individual soul to God and the universe and this poem examines the idea again. It is related to two other central images of growing importance – those of the night sky and the window. You will see in the poetry of Elizabeth Jennings that both symbols are also used as instruments of self-analysis.

The poem is a duologue between the speaker and a summer breeze. Brontë's poem is a rare instance of her describing a precise location, here the garden at Howarth and the rose trees wet with dew as seen through the parlour window. The soft breeze seems like a revivifying power that animates the trees and flowers but at first the speaker rejects its influence. The *Wanderer* (25) persists, wooing the poet with warm, tender kisses yet also reminding her that after death it may sound a less happy note.

Look carefully at the rhyme scheme. Note that all the end-stopped rhymes are monosyllabic while the non-rhyming endings have a double syllable. This regular rhythm creates a gentle, rocking movement.

> 26   **kiss**   there are numerous references to the tender affections – *gentle* (17), *wooing* (18), *sighed* (27).This is a means of making an inanimate object almost human so that the night-wind becomes a confidante, almost a lover.

'There let thy bleeding branch atone'

There is a bitter, almost savage tone to this poem and it may be worth noting that it was written when the poet was contemplating leaving the liberty of Haworth for the 'prison' of schooling in Brussels where she knew she would have little time for poetry. She had written prolifically throughout 1839 (37 poems), developing her interest in doomed Satanic characters which prefigure Heathcliff and finding a personal voice. But she was growing ever more reclusive and this poem registers a new anguish – the theme of self-punishment.

There is a rich legacy of 'broken branches' in literature and mythology but Janet Gezari mentions a possibly more personal connection. As a child, Emily Brontë once crawled out of her bedroom window into the branches of a fruit tree and broke one of the boughs. She was able to confess the offence only on her death-bed. (*Complete Poems of Emily Brontë*, p.282.) One of her best drawings is of a pine-tree with a shattered trunk and broken branch. In her novel, Lockwood dreams of a fir branch tapping at the window of Wuthering Heights which becomes in his dream a child's bleeding wrist. Charlotte too seems to have had a fondness for this image of a broken tree. It is a powerful symbol of divided love in *Jane Eyre*.

> 1   **There let thy bleeding branch atone** a dramatic opening line evoking images of mutilation, self-amputation and sacrifice. How significant is the word order? Note the extremes of emotion and language in the poem: *bleeding* (1), *cursed* (5), *bliss* (8), *wildering* (9), *mad* (10). What effects do these words have on the tone of the poem? Look particularly at the use of allitera-

tion. (See Approaches, p.224 and p.226, for more on Brontë's use of the themes of suffering and attonement in her poems.)

'I see around me tombstones grey'

Although it is usual to associate this poem with Haworth churchyard, it is one of the Gondal series of poems (see p.1) and records the grief of two mourners at their mother's grave. Earth appears grieving for mankind, but death does not destroy human affection (see Elizabeth Jennings' handling of this theme in *It Is Not True?* [p.81]). Torn between fond memories of earth and hopes of eternal rest, Brontë has faith that Nature will not be at the last divided from spirit but reconciled with it. The *dazzling land above* (35), the *Sweet land of light* (15) is too bright for human eyes and seems almost irrelevant to a realm of *boundless misery* (30). The earth bears a human face, a 'mother's' for which we yearn even in the hour of death, striving in *Our last dear longings* (38) to trace *thy darling face* (40). The idea of lost domestic bliss and the mother/child fixation continued to haunt her.

The poem suggests that immortality is not a single but a shared redemption. The symbol of light takes on a more mystical function looking forward to a more complex significance in *The Philosopher* (p.12), *Stars* (p.17) and *The Prisoner* (p.19) her last great poems. You may notice a paradox in the poem. We find her yearning for some supra-terrestrial state yet here she states that earth is her only possible home.

13–14   This view that the traditional idea of heaven affords no solace reminds us of Catherine's dream in *Wuthering Heights* in which she felt that

> **heaven did not seem to be my home; and I broke my heart with weeping to come back to earth; and the angels were so angry that they flung me out, into the middle of the heath on the top of Wuthering Heights; where I woke sobbing for joy. (Chapter 9)**

18   **cell**   the grave.
20   Madness was something the poet feared not merely for herself, but for her brother Branwell whose heavy drinking, addiction to opium and sexual improprieties were a continuing source of shame to the family.

35 **dazzling** see *The Philosopher* lines 35–36 (p.13) for another reference to the dazzling light of the super-human world.

40 **clouded gaze** Brontë's mother had died when the poet was a child. The idea suggests either a dimly remembered past or vision disturbed by excessive light.

The Philosopher

This poem seems like a communication between a poet (seer) and a philosopher, perhaps the two sides of Brontë herself. It marks a moment when one begins to see the emergence of her clairvoyant powers. Juliet Barker, however, in her biography, *The Brontës*, rejects the idea that this poem shows *mystical* vision and suggests it is rather an *externalizing* of imagination. She sees these statements as static, that they did not *inhabit her head but were played out before her as if they were creations independent of her control* (p.482).

This poem rejects the favourite four line stanza for stanzas of an uneven length. Note in particular the poet's punctuation and the copious use of exclamation and question marks to create a sense of close personal engagement with the ideas and feelings.

In content the strong influence of Coleridge is detected. It is a meditation upon the discussions between the metaphysician and the artist and Brontë might be thinking of Coleridge himself. Certainly his two great poems *The Rime of the Ancient Mariner* and *Kubla Khan* are echoed throughout. The conflict here is between being and thinking, the *sentient soul* (52) and the *will* (53). It reveals the emergence of Brontë's quietist philosophy (see Notes to '*I'm happiest when most away*', p.130), the longing for a state *without identity* (8) but at the same time it rejects this option as cowardly and yearns for some 'direct' vision of God. Brontë may have been influenced also by two mystical writers, Swedenborg and Boëhme. Boëhme in his work *Aurora* supports the theory of creation springing from light. Light is a central symbol for Brontë too, second only to love in its power to fuse reason with imagination.

8 **without indentity** this echoes Wordsworth's idea of the grave as *a lonely bed without sense or sight … where we in waiting lie (Ode on the Intimations of Immortality from Recollections of Early Childhood*, [122–124].)

9   **steep**   soak.

10-14   Note the familiar contrast between snow and fire. The word *quenchless* (13) is unusual, meaning here a thirst which can never be assuaged and has overtones of hell-fire.

17   **Three gods**   these may be the Trinity or the threefold man – body, soul and spirit. In stanza four these are referred to as three rivers, gold, blood and sapphire.

27   **I saw a spirit, standing, man**   close to Coleridge's line in *The Rime of the Ancient Mariner: A man all light, a seraph man* (490).

31   **blood**   close to Coleridge's line *The bloody Sun (The Rime of the Ancient Mariner* [112]). See also Brontë's reference to the rising sun *Blood-red, he rose* (21) in *Stars* (p.17).

34   **an inky sea**   this may correspond to Coleridge's *sunless sea* (5) in *Kubla Khan* – a metaphor for death.

39-40   This reference to pure white light which when divided (refracted) becomes the colours of the spectrum takes on a mystical implication. The poet sees colour almost as the 'suffering' of light in some moral battle with darkness. Such pure light is close to Shelley's image of *the white radiance of Eternity* (463) in *Adonais*, another profound influence on this poem. It is not denied to mortal men but its light is 'dazzling'. Humanity's sufferings 'divide' this light and create the beauty and colour of life. Brontë had deep suspicions about purely scientific theories of creation. Both Duffy and Jennings have interesting ideas about the nature of light; see *The Grammar of Light* (p.100) and *The Diamond Cutter* (p.72).

45   **glorious eye**   is Brontë perhaps referring to the eye of God here? The eyes as the *windows of the soul* are referred to in *Wuthering Heights*. She repeats the image in line 5 of *Stars* (p.17).

46   **wilder**   drive insane.

47   See *'No coward soul is mine'* (p.20) where there is a direct confrontation with *Heaven's glories* (3).

49   A rejection of the longing for oblivion or the death-wish and a cultivation of a passive state of contemplation.

Remembrance

This poem belongs to the Gondal sequence. Rosina of Alcona recalls her early love for Julius Brenzaida, Prince of Angora. The Gondal names have been removed but this does not diminish the intense, personal emotion. Here is perhaps Brontë's most mature and successful working of the theme of Romantic love as the union of twin-souls. As such it recalls the anguished, divided love of Catherine and Heathcliff. As in *Death* (p.15), the death-wish is restrained as the poet succeeds in transcending mere nostalgia and learns to live without remembrance.

Look most carefully at the structure of the poem. The line is predominantly iambic pentameter but is made more dynamic by stressing the first syllable of each line – *Cold* (1), *Far* (2), *Sweet* (13), *All* (19) and by a caesura, or slight pause after the second foot. This is particularly striking in the first four stanzas. A driving tempo suggests urgency and passion, the caesura defining a moment of breathless, breaking emotion. When your ear is sufficiently tuned to Brontë's poetry you will recognize this insistent energy as part of her great originality. Note how she makes use of repetition, to suggest ever-returning pain.

4   **all-severing**   dividing, another of her compound adjectives.

6   **northern shore**   in the 'Gondal Poems Notebook', Angora's shore. Angora is one of the kingdoms of Gondal.

7   **heath and fern-leaves**   the grave of the beloved is set in an isolated landscape, heath or moorland. Has he returned to a primal state of nature? Compare this with *A Farewell to Alexandria* (p.6). (See Notes, p.132.)

9–10   **fifteen wild Decembers**   this belongs to a Gondal chronology – it is 15 years since the death of Brenzaida – and is a striking way of marking the passage of time. The later word *melted* (10) has associations with a thawing of stubborn grief into the tears mentioned in line 25.

13   **sweet Love of youth**   recalls first love and the idea of the loved one returning to the universal pulse of nature. Do you notice any possible associations with *Romeo and Juliet* in this poem?

23–24   The 'stoic' attitude – see Notes to *'No coward soul is mine'* (p.142).

28 The morbid but fascinating idea expressed in this line is repeated in *Wuthering Heights* where Heathcliff arranges for his coffin to be buried alongside Catherine's.

32 Five out of the eight stanzas end on either a question mark or exclamation mark. You may want to think about this poem in dramatic terms, as a monologue.

Death

You will notice throughout the selection the poet's preoccupation with themes of burial and early death. This poem is a virtual invitation to *strike again* (3) and shows a strange, masochistic need to suffer. Like other poems it is built around a series of opposites – exhilaration and revival with its references to *fresh* (4), *dew* (6), *pride* (10), *restoring* (12), *winged* (21) with the contrary images of despondency and extinction – *droop* (25), *languish* (25), *mouldering* (31). The entire poem is an extended metaphor of a sapling assailed by changing seasons and the arbitrary moods of the weather. It may recall the words of Christ: *I am the vine and ye are the branches. If a man abide not in me, he is cast forth as a branch and is withered.* (John,15,5–6.) Finally the speaker accepts and even rejoices in defeat. Writing of her sister's own death in 1848 Charlotte Brontë employed the metaphor of the tree. She was, she wrote *like a tree in full bearing – struck at the root.* (Juliet Barker, *The Brontës*, p.579.)

Look carefully at the poet's verbal technique. Some verbs are violent: *struck* (1), *plucked* (9), *stripped* (10), but others are passive and tender: *confiding* (1), *whispering* (16), *caressing* (19). It is possible to recognize erotic and sexual implications. It may be significant that death is seen as a cruel lover who invites trust and confession but responds first with blows, then disease and finally extinction.

1 **confiding** trusting in someone to whom one makes a secret confession. Death comes as a sudden blow made more cruel by the victim's innocence.

3 Note again Brontë's reference to the cutting of a branch (see *'There let thy bleeding branch atone'*, p.10) and the suggestion of self-torture.

4–8 The poet describes a harmonious ecological balance in nature not repeated in human life.

9-12   Sorrow and guilt strip away external beauty but hope (sap) continues to flow.

18   **beauty-burdened** nature brings an over abundance of blossom in cruel mockery of the final fate.

24   **blight** a disease associated with plants. Brontë was writing before Darwin but her view of 'growing' souls has similarities with evolutionary theory and the idea of the survival of the fittest. Darwin also states that diseases in natural forms are a positive force of adaption.

26   Does this imply a last, desperate hope of survival?

27   The poet identifies herself with the tree at this point.

32   **Eternity** the word does not imply insensibility, as in some of Dickinson's poems, but a confidence and trust in God. Brontë was fond of ending her poems with this abstract noun almost as something which sweeps away doubt and despair.

Stars

Stars furthers the poet's interest in light – here starlight, renewing the image of the *glorious eye* (45) from *The Philosopher* (p.14). Brontë appears to have kept watch all night, enraptured by the stars' gentle influence. But now the sky becomes a *desert* (4) as the sun's *fierce beams* (22) put the stars to flight. This vulgar, intrusive blaze floods her bedroom. Night seemed a time for dreams, for peaceful reverie and branching thoughts. Day brings a stark reality which *does not warm, but burn* (44).

9-10   The reference here to drinking light as if it were some life-giving power has strong associations again with Coleridge's *The Rime of the Ancient Mariner*. The mariner, surrounded by the corpses of his fellow sailors watches the stars. By their light he sleeps and 'drinks' the dew of God's grace. Brontë continues to develop ideas on light explored in *The Philosopher* (p.12).

12   **petrel** a small sea bird with black and white plumage and long wings often associated with stormy weather. The bird continues the association with Coleridge's poem and the albatross. Note that Plath also employs bird imagery in *Black Rook in Rainy Weather* (p.37) and *A Winter Ship* (p.38) in a spiritual context.

13-16   This stanza describes an almost trance-like state of meditation.

19-20   Note the familiar opposites *scorch with fire* (19) and *cool radiance* (20).

21 **Blood-red, he rose** a striking line perhaps developing thoughts on blood in *The Philosopher* (p.12).

29 **I turned me to the pillow** see Elizabeth Jennings' poem *In the Night* (p.67). We learn that Brontë died *turning her dying eyes reluctantly from the pleasant sun.* (Juliet Barker, *The Brontës*, p.576.)

37 **wakened flies** the image is of insects which have been imprisoned until the speaker opens the window. See also Dickinson's *'I heard a Fly buzz – when I died'* (p.29).

45–46 There is a hint of the vampire in these lines but Brontë transforms the image and portrays the sun as a pitiless being that exposes the stark realities of day.

The Prisoner

A narrator and jailor visits a dungeon to speak with the female prisoner who describes that state of the soul when it transcends the merely physical and attains a state of divine vision. There are two distinct schools of thought about this poem. One is that these lines show the poet's mystic powers in the manner of St Teresa of Avila or St John of the Cross, both Christian mystics who described their personal sense of union with God; the other confines the poem to its Gondal background. It has become unfashionable to relate Brontë's work entirely to herself. In relating her poetry directly to her life we must remember that no theory is capable of final proof. But perhaps the Gondal research movement has gone too far in insisting that the poems must be confined only to a local and narrow culture. The poet herself extracted this section from the longer work and adapted it for separate publication. C. Day Lewis has described these lines as among the finest mystical writing in the English language. It certainly escapes the restrictions of the Gondal world where often the tone is melodramatic and the writing sometimes mediocre. What is so impressive is the way the poet has gathered together and distilled so many powerful feelings and thoughts, into a unified pattern.

The poem reveals a remarkable individual; reclusive, obsessive, defiant and at this point in her life in the first stages of consumption. It recalls an earlier poem *'And first an hour of mournful musing'* with its six stages of revelation (see Notes, p.130) but taken two further stages into spiritual rapture and the sense of imminent liberty – *Its wings are almost free* (15) – to the final restraint of physicality. There remains a last and final realization which accords with that masochistic side of the poet we have seen elsewhere: *The more that anguish racks, the earlier it will bless* (22).

1   Why western winds? The answer might lie in her love of the Romantic poet Shelley whose *Ode to the West Wind* was a formative influence. Perhaps a west wind is associated with spring, warmth and a reviving of the spirits. (See *The Night-Wind*, p.9.)

2   **thickest**   how appropriate do you think the word is to describe stars? Perhaps the poet associates the stars with spring blossoms on orchard boughs referred to also in *Death* (p.15).

7   **flashes warm**   like *dazzle* and *blaze* the poet shows a fondness for this particular tone-colour. She was also fascinated by opposites such as cold/heat, light/dark.

14   **my inward essence**   the core of her being.

15   **Its wings are almost free**   the image suggests a butterfly escaping from the chrysalis. The poet had written in one of her Brussels' essays, *Le Papillon* of 1842, *Just as the ugly caterpillar is the origin of the splendid butterfly so this world is the embryo of a new heaven.*

17–20   The insistent energy of this stanza shows the poet at her best. Note how the rhythm powerfully stresses the important words in a chain of thought *ear* (18), *eye* (18), *pulse* (19), *brain* (19), *soul* (20), *flesh* (20), *chain* (20) describing an almost unbearable disappointment as the soul is arrested in its flight, is increasingly restrained by the senses until it finally reels under the check of its physical chain. The harsh image of the iron chain drastically contrasts with the spiritual lightness of the butterfly's wing.

23   **robed in fires**   a wonderful combination of images associated with the inferno or hell.

'No coward soul is mine'

This poem was to be the last Emily Brontë thought worthy of transcribing into her fair copy notebook and shows her at the height of her poetic power. It is perhaps her most famous poem and has been set to music as a Victorian hymn but it is not overtly Christian in content and is in many ways a contradiction to those earlier poems which yearn for oblivion.

Classical in style, it is neither impersonal nor cold. It is a triumphant declaration of faith but it is also a rejection of conventional Christian values. It is Christian in spirit but not in idea. It is closer perhaps to old fashioned Deism or natural religion – a belief in the existance of a supreme being, but one which rejects direct revelation – than belief in the Trinity – Father, Son and Holy Ghost. Critics, like May Sinclair, (*The Three Brontës*) have objected to a rather *frigid* Deism. This is also reflected in more scientific allusions – *animates* (18), *dissolves* (20), *atom* (26), *void* (26), *suns and universes* (22) – surprising ones given the poet's suspicions about the purely physical sciences.

The quality of the poem lies in its absolute conviction. Its belief in 'life' both physical and spiritual is implied in the very first line and continues until the last confident statement. God is seen as an indestructible force which blows through the universe leaving no room for contradiction. Brontë adopts her favourite four line stanza as a simple but strong meditation for these emphatic active verbs which are so characteristic. This is seen particularly well in stanza five where she piles one upon another in her description of some vast creative force which animates all forms and finally sweeps death aside. The philosophical heart of the poem is in stanzas one and two which seem a personal statement of belief in her own spiritual identity. Succeeding stanzas move away from self into a consideration of God.

2   **trembler**   one shaken by doubt. The word hints at the Quaker faith. The Tremblers were a branch of Puritanism believing in the direct intervention of God.

9   **creeds**   a set of principles which act as a philosophy for life.

12   **froth**   foam, bubbles upon water. The poet rejects consolation that is merely intellectual as worthless.

13–16   The image is of faith as a rock surrounded by the spume and spray of the sea.

16   **steadfast rock**   perhaps St Peter, the rock of the Christian church.

19   **pervades**   to pass through, diffuses itself throughout.

20   **rears**   a vague word probably chosen to rhyme with *years* (18) but may imply something lifted up out of ignominy. Also used in *Paradise Lost* to describe Satan rising from the burning lake.

24   All human souls reside in God.

26   **void**   empty, a vacuum.

Poems by Emily Dickinson

'Success is counted sweetest'

We used to think . . . that words were cheap and weak. Now I don't know of anything so mighty. There are [those] to which I lift my hat when I see them sitting princelike among their peers on the page. Sometimes I write one, and look at his outlines till he glows as no sapphire. (*The Lyman Letters*, Richard B. Sewall, p.78)

Dickinson defines *Victory* (8) by describing an occasion when it occurs, claiming that someone who has engaged in an experience is best fitted to *comprehend* (3) it. *Success* (1), the opening word, appears to be the key term but her concern is with failure. Consider the negatives *ne'er* (2), *Not one* (5), *defeated* (9) and *forbidden* (10). Insistently they throw doubt on the value of *Success* (1) as she asserts that a fuller understanding of *Victory* (8) belongs to those who experience its opposite, defeat.

    3   **nectar**   sweet drink enjoyed by classical Gods.
    5   **purple**   the Romans used an expensive purple dye to colour the Emperor's robes. It came to symbolize royalty. The victorious army *Host* wear the colour of worldly success.
  10   **forbidden**   what is forbidden? Is it *Victory* (8) which turns out to be the price of comprehension? If so, if the dying man is on his way to the Elysian fields, it suggests that Dickinson scarcely values worldly *Success* (1). Yet the poem's final line registers powerfully the pain of *those who ne'er succeed* (2).

'South Winds jostle them'

It was a familiar gesture of Dickinson to send flowers to friends with a note or verse attached. The tone of the poem is affectionate and caring and the flowers are pictured at the centre of seductive and nourishing activity. What is the effect of the verbs in the poem?

    6   **Cashmere**   brightly patterned shawls from the Kashmir region of India were costly garments. As the only unusual word

amongst simple vocabulary, *Cashmere* hints at an exotic luxury which contrasts with the domesticity of the poem's occasion and suggests a richness in the gift exceeding its apparent ordinariness.

7   **softly plucking**   the adverb describes the personal involvement of the speaker as a careful act. What other words sustain the mood of gentleness?

'Safe in their Alabaster Chambers'

Two balanced stanzas juxtapose the inert state of the untroubled dead, resting peacefully or passively in their stone tombs, with the ceaseless activity of the natural world above them. One view is from inside the tomb, looking up at *Rafter* and *Roof* (5). The other view is external, encompassing the sweep of the galaxies and the time span of history. Safely tucked into their tombs, the dead rest *Untouched* (2) by the *Grand* (6) passage of time.

Does the celebratory tone of the second stanza imply that the dead are missing out on wondrous events? Consider the verbs. In the first stanza there is only one, the inert *lie* (4). The second stanza has active verbs: *go* (6), *scoop* (7), *row* (8), *drop* (9), *surrender* (9). Stillness and activity, meekness and grandeur, security and loss, inclusion and exclusion; the alternatives pile up in ways which question whether the *meek members of the Resurrection* (4) in their rich rooms of *Alabaster* (1) and *Satin* (5) have the poet's approval. How *Safe* (1) are the dead?

1   **Chambers**   a private room or bedroom. It introduces the sustained image of the dead inhabiting a rich house.

4   **the meek members of the Resurrection**   at the *Resurrection* God summons the dead to rise from their graves and be judged. Here the dead wait meekly but should they be so certain of salvation? Could Dickinson be mocking the expectations of pious Puritans who believed that their faith guaranteed them a place in Heaven?

5   **Rafter of Satin**   the coffin lining?
Roof of Stone   tombstone?

8   **row**   suggests the skies moving, like the dipping blades of oars, in arcs above the stillness of the stone tomb.

9 **Doges**   Doges were the rulers of Venice, the beautiful, Italian, maritime trading city at the crossroads of East and West, associated with luxury and privilege. Does the line carry the sense that wealth and power cannot last? Cannot protect?

10   Some critics argue that the image, although apparently of a winter countryside, cannot be visualized. Can dots be *Soundless?* Or snow a *Disc?* At the end of the poem there is a sensuous fading away into a silent, viewless, ungraspable absence.

'Over the fence'

The speaking voice of a young child is delightfully conveyed in this poem by short phrases, repetitions and simple vocabulary. The broken syntax reveals the child's hesitation between the temptation of climbing the fence or remaining a good, dutiful girl in a clean apron.

This poem's conflict pivots on the word *But* (6) which changes the assertiveness of a young girl, confident of her climbing ability and doubtful of God's *if He could!* (9), into a daughter's reluctant obedience to a restrictive, rule-enforcing father. In her recognition that God would probably climb if he were a *Boy* (8), that adulthood is less fun than childhood *Oh, dear* (8), is this a poem about resigned acceptance of the rules that God and/or fathers have set? Or is it a poem of proud defiance?

'There's a certain Slant of light'

At first this appears to be a nature poem describing the effect of light on a winter's afternoon. At what point do you realize that it is more than a realistic picture?

As in Plath's *Black Rook in Rainy Weather* (p.37) something unworldly is happening. Grammatically the subject of the poem is *Despair* (10) and Dickinson claims that the feeling is universal. It comes to *us* (5). *We* (6) study its effects. In the last stanza the weight of *Despair* (10) extends to touch the natural world which responds to a revelation which seems to have been sent to warn us. Personified nature holds its breath (13-14) so we cannot doubt this is a momentous visitation. The final simile links *Distance* (15) and *Death* (16) in ways which are teasingly unclear. Do corpses look as though they are staring into the distance? Is Dickinson personifying Death? Or have we momentarily glimpsed our own death which we normally keep at a *Distance* (15)?

1   **Slant of light**   may suggest the way light falls into the nave of a cathedral from the high celestory windows but grammatically it relates to *Winter Afternoons* (2). Why slanted? Is there a sense of light falling directly from heaven?

3   **Heft**   weight. The slightly archaic word adds to the heavy mood set by the winter afternoon and the cathedral music.

9   **Any**   the word is left hanging. It is not grammatically linked into the sentence. Does it relate to *None* in the sense that no one, not a single person may teach? Does it relate to the reader, no one can teach any of us? Does it relate to *it* (9); no one can teach any thing? As so often, Dickinson's ambiguous grammar and idiosyncratic punctuation leave the interpretation open.

10   **Seal Despair**   the metaphor comparing *Despair* to a *Seal*, whether on a document or a closed room or box, has an impressive and weighty feel, suggesting that despair stamps its mark on us with legal finality.

11   **imperial affliction**   why should *affliction* be *imperial?* Does *Despair* (10) descend upon us inescapably or is it sent by command? Like *Heft* (3) the word conveys a sense of gravity, awe and solemnity.

'I'm Nobody! Who are you?'

This is an example of Dickinson's mocking, humorous attitude towards authority, power, and status. She denies value to any activity which wins public applause. You may feel a sense of gender roles in the *Somebody* (5)/*Nobody* (2) opposition.

'The Soul selects her own Society'

The poem dignifies a human being by valuing her choice of lover. Discrimination and fidelity reflect back onto the chooser so that the personal qualities of the chosen one are irrelevant. It is the act of choosing and remaining faithful which gives worth and the absolute nature of the decision is conveyed in images of enclosure. The chooser is seen as a lowly, disempowered housewife whose modest, homely possessions *Door* (2), *low Gate* (6), and *Mat* (8) contrast with the rich, regal trappings *Chariots* (5) of the suitors. She is her own *Majority* (3) and the religious terms which describe her, *Soul* (1), *divine* (3) assert her superiority and independence.

- 1 **selects** the first of a series of verbs associated with the Soul. Others are *shuts* (2), *notes* (5), *Choose* (10) and *close* (11). Notice how decisive they are. They help to establish the image of the Soul as a woman in control.
- 11 **Valves** a strikingly industrial image in the context of the poem. Another version of the poem reads *lid*, a less unusual image of enclosure. *Valves* is an unexpected word, perhaps conveying a tighter sense of being shut off?

'A Bird came down the Walk'

The quick movements of the bird as he warily feeds are conveyed in the first half of the poem with its sharp observation, simple vocabulary, and end-stopped lines. When the poet tentatively offers a crumb, he takes flight in a series of abstract images which seem to give a blessing to an otherwise comical and natural portrayal of the bird.

- 4 **fellow, raw** the comradely use of *fellow* is immediately juxtaposed with the shock of the word *raw*. How do you feel about this? There is no hint in the off-hand tone at the opening that the mood will change to wonder at the end.
- 6 **convenient** the adjective continues the sense that the bird enjoys the advantages of a privileged position in the natural world.
- 9–13 These lines reveal that nature is not as safe for the bird as the opening stanzas suggested. The adjectives *rapid* (9) and *frightened* (11) and the verbs *glanced* (9), *hurried* (10) and *stirred* (12) alert the reader to an awareness of his danger.
- 13 **Cautious** it is unclear whether the adjective qualifies the bird or the speaker. Ambiguity blurs any distinction between them.
- 16 **home** safety, and home, are not to be found on the *Walk* (1).
- 15–20 As the bird takes flight, the plain language of precise, scientific observation shifts to abstract metaphors (the bird *rowed* [16], butterflies *Leap* [20] off *Banks of Noon* [19]) which transform our relationship to the natural world. Suddenly it is not a place of dangerous survival but of startling, supernatural beauty.

'After great pain, a formal feeling comes'

Dickinson wrote a series of poems about the act of continuing to live after a catastrophic, emotional blow, a state which the critic David Porter has aptly named *living in the aftermath*. (*Dickinson: The Modern Idiom*, p.9.) (See also '*We grow accustomed to the Dark*', p.28, '*Immortal is an ample word*', p.31, '*My life closed twice before its close*', p.32 and '*Elysium is as far as to*', p.33.) Stiff, mechanical imagery pervades this poem. She draws upon wood, stone, quartz and lead before culminating with a picture of *persons* (12) freezing into the ceremonial tomb-figures with which the poem opens.

3   **He**   in Dickinson's idiosyncratic punctuation capital letters cannot be trusted to carry any particular significance, but this could refer to Christ.

6   **Ought**   the syntax suggests that Dickinson is using the word as a noun, indicating a place like *Ground* and *Air* in which the body continues to operate in a dazed, dutiful, mechanical way. In this reading, the *Feet* (5) move in a physical space *Ground*, a mental space *Air* and a metaphorical space *Ought* where only a sense of habitual obligation drives the person to continue living. However, *Ought* could mean 'anything' or 'anywhere' in which case the line seems to mean that while people go on living after great emotional loss, on earth, in air or anywhere, existence is meaningless.

13   **letting go**   the phrase can be read as the last stage, following *Chill* and *Stupor*, in the numbing process which reduces a human to the state of an unfeeling tomb. Or it can be read more actively, the *letting-go* of *Chill* and *Stupor* and thus the act of rejecting a numbing loss of feeling by reasserting the power of the human will to decide, even if it is a decision to accept failure.

'We grow accustomed to the Dark'

This is another poem where Dickinson describes the effect of a momentous event which changes a person's life. Her usual reaction to the devastating blow is withdrawal into a kind of frozen cessation of feeling. Here she presents the moment when life alters in an amused, optimistic way, using the sustained image of someone stumbling as they leave a neighbour's house after dark.

1 **Dark**   do you think the word is being used realistically, symbolically or both?

20 **straight**   stoical endurance is this poet's normal reaction to loss or defeat. Notice how *straight* links with *erect* (8). In this poem *Life* is personified as someone who gropes and bumps into trees, who *Adjusts* (19) and becomes *accustomed* (1) to change. There is jauntiness in the qualifying adverb *almost*. Wry humour suggests a victory for *Life* which is unusual in her poems of loss.

'I heard a Fly buzz – when I died'

The *King* (7) whose coming everyone in the room waits to witness could be either death or God. It makes no difference to the solemnity of the *last Onset* (7). But for the dying person the buzz of a fly intrudes, distracting his or her attention. The tone of the poem is not irritable. Nor does the mundane intrusion deflate a sacramental occasion. It is difficult to pinpoint the effect of juxtaposing the sacred and the profane. Is the presence of so ordinary a creature as a fly a reminder of the triviality of the daily world which is being shed at the supreme moment of revelation? Or is there fellow-feeling with one of the smallest of God's creatures, a shared sense of uncertainty about what lies beyond the light? The poem leaves us as mystified as the narrator.

7 **Onset**   start, beginning, in the sense of the start of an attack or assault.

8 **witnessed**   who is doing the witnessing and what do they witness? Is the after-life being revealed to the dying person or are the mourners witnessing death?

9 **willed ... Signed away**   the legal terms lend formality to the shedding of possessions *Keepsakes* (i.e. loved but not valuable objects) and the human body or whatever *portion* (10) is felt not to be already owned by another, presumably God.

13 **uncertain stumbling**   do the adjectives refer only to the *Fly* (12) or does the dying person share in the uncertainty? The words seem to point forward to the last line.

14 **light**   this could mean any of the following: daylight; consciousness; life.

15 **Windows**   windows in the room which are fading as sight dims? It could also mean eyes or soul.

'Because I could not stop for Death'

The humorous arrogance of the opening line strikes a naive note which starts the poem in a deceptively simple style. The speaker seems ingenuous and willing to enter the carriage even though it is unclear whether Death is recognized or a stranger since his mannerly behaviour promises safety: he *kindly* (2) stopped, he drives with *no haste* (5). Death is personified as a courteous gentleman taking a lady companion on a leisurely carriage drive out of town, into the countryside and beyond. You might find it helpful to think about the place and time markers in the poem. Indications of where the carriage is heading are precise and local at the start: *School* (9) and *Fields* (11) but at the end the setting is unlocated and unrealized. When does the narrator become aware that her journey may be more than an afternoon's outing?

Her understanding begins to alter at *Or rather – He passed Us* (13). The strange *House* (17) gives her pause. If the *Swelling of the Ground* (18) is a grave and the *Roof* (19) and *Cornice* (20) a tombstone, they function smoothly as a transition between the body's realistic journey to the town's burial ground and the soul's journey to *Eternity* (24). But are the events happening so seamlessly or has a whole lifetime been condensed into a single afternoon? Indications of time are the schoolchildren playing *At Recess* (10) which could be a morning break, the *Gazing Grain* (11) with its sense of midday or afternoon heat, the *Setting Sun* (12) and finally the evening *Dews* (14) for which she is too lightly clad. We start by assuming the events are taking place on the same day until the final verse shifts us, startlingly, into a completely different time scale where *Centuries* (21) count for nothing.

Death can be seen as a lover or a father-figure. The romantic implications of a courting couple in a carriage which *held but just Ourselves* (3) are kept in check by the alternative reading where Death is the driver, the experienced mentor gently conveying the innocent girl into new experiences. The possibility of underlying erotic meanings have led to feminist readings that take the poem to be about marriage as a kind of death.

Because Death is identified at the outset we are immediately made aware of the metaphorical nature of the journey, but the narrator herself appears innocent and the poem plays with complementary and contradictory ideas of courtship and funeral, innocence and knowledge. Holding the balance of these ambiguities creates a tension throughout the poem between the social civilities of genteel behaviour and the unmentionable enormity of what is happening. When the narrator begins to register the true direction of her journey her tone remains calm; she only *surmised* (23), offering possibilities that her guess could be wrong. Yet there is a *chill* (14) in the poem, indicated in the *quivering* approach of the *Dews* (14). *Feels* (22) is in the present tense. How does she feel and has she completed her journey?

- 4 **Immortality** sophisticated Latinate words contrast with the plain vocabulary in the rest of the poem. Notice also *Civility* (8) and *Eternity* (24). These words, placed tellingly at the ends of stanzas, sum up the tension between the courtesy and reality of death.
- 10 **Recess** break, playtime.
- 11 **Gazing Grain** does the grain turn to gaze at the sun, a description which would suggest a pastoral scene in golden daylight? Or does it gaze at the passing carriage, like crowds witnessing an important event?
- 15 **Gossamer** a gauzy, silky fabric of the filmiest, fine texture.
- 16 **Tippet** a woman's cape, usually made of fur not *Tulle* (16), a flimsy fabric. As a lightly-clad passenger, she feels the chill of evening; as a dying person, the chill of approaching death. Is there a hint of burial cloths wrapping her corpse? The delicacy of the feminine fabrics continues the illusion of a genteel drive and eases the moment of death.
- 20 **Cornice** moulding at the roof of a building. The *House* (17), only partly visible above the earth, could be a burial tomb. It is the only time on the journey when the carriage, apart from stopping to pick her up, makes a pause. Why might this be?
- 23 **surmised** guessed. The penultimate verb maintains to the end a sense of uncertainty about the nature of the journey and its destination.

'Presentiment – is that long Shadow – on the Lawn'

As with *'Success is counted sweetest'* (p.23), Dickinson tries to define a word, *Presentiment*, by describing an experience, the coming of nightfall. The second couplet expands upon the description, taking us from an ordinary sight to an intangible experience; from a physical activity to a mental one. In the process the attempt to fix meaning is undermined. What are we being given notice of and why should it startle the grass? Is it nightfall, or something graver?

Notice the shift in tone between the leisurely opening line and the short, sharp, later lines. What starts as neutral statement changes to foreboding. Tranquility is disturbed; security shifts to uncertainty; a simple occurrence hints at eternity.

1. **Presentiment** one of only two sophisticated words in the poem. The sense that this is a weighty word is conveyed also by its position at the head of the poem.
2. **Indicative** stating, declaring.
3. **Notice** who is giving notice? Nature or God?
   startled is the grass *startled* because it has no awareness of time or memory of nightfall, unlike humans. Or is a greater event of magnitude about to happen? The unexpected adjective is disquieting.
4. **Darkness** what is passing? Is it daylight – or a warning of death?

'Finding is the first Act'

In this poem, Dickinson treats her familiar theme of the change which follows disappointment more light-heartedly. Here, each step of the search for the lost, precious thing leads to the progressive discovery that it was not worth prizing in the first place. Experience brings nothing but mounting distrust. What do you think the word *too* (8) in the final line relates to? What else is *sham* (8)?

4. **Golden Fleece** the classical Greek hero *Jason* (8) sailed with 50 warriors, named the Argonauts after their ship the Argos, to find the fabled Golden Fleece which hung in a sacred grove in Colchis. Initially, Jason appeared successful. He won the Golden Fleece and regained his father's kingdom which had been the impelling reason for his quest, but the remainder of his life was inconspicuous and mundane.

'Immortal is an ample word'

The poem starts deceptively, describing the word *Immortal* (1) as *ample* (1) with comfortable connotations of large size and abundant time. All too soon the familar *But* (3) alerts us to the true direction of the poem, which is to define something by its absence. We begin to understand *Heaven* (8) only when we have lost it.

> 7   **its**   refers to *Heaven* in line 5.
>   **marauding**   raiding; robbing and killing at will, indiscrimately.

'The Show is not the Show'

The poem starts by bluntly denying the normal meaning of the word *Show* (1) before substituting Dickinson's private, humorous redefinition. If spectators, *they that go* (2), have become the *Show* (1), who is now the spectator?

> 4   **My Neighbour**   why has Dickinson used the singular noun? Is it a collective noun and has all the world become a *Show* (1) to her?
> 5   **Fair Play**   the colloquial exclamation defiantly stakes her right to see life independently and differently.

'Apparently with no surprise'

In this poem Nature is taken unawares and the frost's acts are *accidental* (4). It is the *Approving God* (8) whom Dickinson accuses and holds responsible for death.

'The Pedigree of Honey'

Many of Dickinson's poems express her delight in the natural world. The light, comical touch of this poem is achieved by the unexpected association of bees with the human hierarchies of breeding, rank, and status. Is there a mocking implication that we would all be happier if we were more appreciative of humble pleasures?

'My life closed twice before its close'

Whether the poem refers to events in Dickinson's personal life or to imagined experiences can never be known but the poem is one of the clearest statements of the devastating effects of loss. The final couplet uses a favourite device, the syntax of the defining statement *Parting is* . . . (7) (see also '*Presentiment – is that long Shadow – on the Lawn*', p.31 and '*Elysium is as far as to*', p.33) and one of her common modes, ambiguity. Our understanding of *heaven* (7) and *hell* (8) arises from the same experience, *Parting* (7). As in '*Success is counted sweetest*' (p.23), we only realize the true meaning of something when we experience its loss.

'To make a prairie it takes a clover and one bee'

The importance of Nature to Dickinson and her contentment with a severely restricted lifestyle are both celebrated in this poem. She reduces an expansive *prairie* (1), that image of fruitful, limitless, pioneering space, to a single clover and a single bee, insisting by repetition that this is sufficient. Then she reduces this even further, rejecting the need for any physical presence at all. Memory and a creative mind *will do* (4). Is this a metaphor for poetry?

3 **revery** a creative daydream.

'Elysium is as far as to'

Footsteps, a door opening; these simple actions carry the weight of a supreme mystery, the transition between life and death. Does the *coming Foot* (7) belong to God or the person attending the dying? As in '*I heard a Fly buzz – when I died*' (p.29) familiar sounds can tug at human consciousness or herald the Soul's entry into the unknown. Does the *Door* (8) open for the poet to receive news or for the dying person to be received into eternity? Remember the poems in which Dickinson attempts to define a chosen word and notice how she uses the same syntactical stucture here *Elysium is* . . . (1). *Elysium* could be joyful news or the destination of the dying. Whose is the *Soul* (5)?

1 **Elysium** heaven in Greek classical mythology.
4 **Felicity** happiness.
 Doom fate, death, the Last Judgement.

'That Love is all there is'

Love (1) is defined by absence, by a refusal to provide any definition and by a defence of that refusal. An authoritative statement is confirmed by the decisive cutting-off of further questioning with the dismissive *It is enough* (3). To the end Dickinson eludes the reader. Does *It is enough* (3) refer to our questioning or to the essential nature of *Love* (1)?

    3-4   **freight ... groove**   whether it refers to a freight train running on grooved wheels or a drawer running on grooved sides, the image conveys a sense of the intimate fit between the weight of Love and the channel which carries it.

Poems by Sylvia Plath

Ode for Ted

In *Ode for Ted* Plath celebrates her early love for Ted Hughes, placing him in the Yorkshire countryside of the Calder Valley where he grew up. Subtle half-rhymes follow a strict pattern. She draws upon the techniques of Anglo Saxon poetry (she was experimenting in the style of Gerard Manley Hopkins); alliteration, abnormal syntax and an absence of prepositions, pronouns or conjunctions. The Anglo Saxon practice of forming descriptive nouns or 'kennings' out of metaphoric phrases inspired her to invent riddling words, like *worm-haunt* (8) for the tunnels moles make in the earth as they hunt for worms. The heavy use of monosyllables gives a feeling of weight and power to the man. His acts are simple, but magnified by her choice of archaic words like *hefting* (9) and *hest* (18). Notice how alive and active the verbs which are associated with him are. He *names* birds(3), *starts* rabbits (3), *stalks* wildlife (6) and *splits* rocks (10). He walks in an aura of creative power.

    4   **nimble**   nimbly, but by making it an adjective rather than an adverb Plath allows the word to fit both the man and his actions.

    9   **hefting chalk-hulled flint**   lifting flints which have been embedded in the chalk. What picture of the man is created by his actions?

    13   **acres yield**   Nature defers at his slightest glance. How do the *oat-sprouts* (2) react? How do *rabbits* (3), *grain* (16) and *birds* (18) behave?

20 **shirr** to gather fabric into pleated rows. Plath is probably referring onomatopoeically to the sound of the ringdoves, cooing together.

21 **saunters** wanders, strolls. He is at ease moving through the natural landscape.

22 **adam's woman** why do you think Plath chooses to associate him with the biblical Adam? And what do you feel about her identifying herself as his possession?

Black Rook in Rainy Weather

If this seems a difficult poem you might like to start by identifying where it changes tone. Lines of curt monosyllables, like the opening lines, move suddenly into flowing lines of smooth polysyllables. The mood of the poem swings violently. It starts in muted despondency. The weather is *desultory* (8), the landscape *dull, ruinous* (24), the domestic setting *obtuse* (18). The poet protests that she expects nothing to happen, not a *miracle* (4) not even an *accident* (5). Yet running beneath her *fear/Of total neutrality* (31-2) do you sense that she hopes *it could happen* (23)? What is the poet hoping for? A *miracle* (4), a *descent* (40)? Its appearance is heralded by light. It is *incandescent* (15), a *celestial burning* (17). It will *set the sight on fire* (6). Notice how the word *shine* (28) which describes the rook *Ordering* (28) its wet feathers echoes these images of light.

At first she seems resigned to the absence of *miracles* (38). *I do not expect* (4), *I can't honestly complain* (13). But she recognizes *now and then* (18) that a *minor light* (14) shines out of the most ordinary domestic objects and that an angel may be at her elbow even though she is ignorant of his presence. The recognition is enough to make her *walk/Wary* (22-23). When the rook arrives there is no doubting his importance. The sight of him seizes her senses and hauls her *eyelids up* (30). Of course she remains suspicious. It could be a trick and she sounds uncertain *If you care to call* (37). But her mood of rejection has changed to a tentative belief that *Miracles occur* (36) and a willingness to wait for the *rare, random descent* (40) whose importance she signifies by giving the phrase a privileged position in the final line.

12 **backtalk** she would like a conversation, or at least a response. At this stage she has not recognized the rook may be a sign from heaven.

    15   **incandescent**   a burning, intensely bright glow.

    21   **largesse**   a generous gift.

    25   **politic**   prudent, suggests wariness, a sense of holding back.

31-36   What creates the *brief respite* (31) and boost in confidence that *With luck* (32) implies? Notice how the phrases *Patch together* (35) and *Of sorts* (36) subtly reduce her *content* (35).

    40   **rare, random descent**   after the death of Christ, the Holy Spirit descended in tongues of fire on the Apostles seated at the feast of Pentecost. They were able to speak many languages. It suggests that the miracle which she longs for may be inspired language. What other things might be a miracle for her?

A Winter Ship

Plath likens the *dull* (13) scene which opens the poem to an *etching* (13) and one could paint it from the details she gives us: *outmoded* (3) barges, *shanty* (6) ridgepoles, *rickety* (16) warehouses and pilings *about to collapse* (15). Nothing is spick and span in contrast to the glittering fragility of the *iceribbed ship* (25). Is it a glimpse of a wilder existence, the *tough weather* (27) beyond the safe *flat harbour* (9)? Is it a sense of freedom, the life of an *albatross* (26) rather than barges *Shackled to the dock* (3)? What of the danger implicit in the final simile? The affection Plath has for seascapes is apparent in this poem but which of the contrasting scenes, the working wharf or the *iceribbed ship* (25), do you think the poet prefers?

    11   **blimp**   round metal cover? inflatable airship?

    19   **vernacular**   the common local language.

    26   **albatross**   is there an allusion to Coleridge's *The Rime of the Ancient Mariner*?

    28   **pellicle**   thin skin. Do you feel the strangeness of the word suits the ship?

Two Views of a Cadaver Room

The poem's title suggests Plath equates the world of war with a dissecting chamber. Both are rooms of death. The stanzas and rhyme scheme (a mixture of half and full rhymes) balance exactly. Plath's view appears disengaged. She steps back, as it were, in the space before each concluding couplet to register her reaction. What moves her? Does it imply a contrast between male and female views?

The surprising gesture of handing her a heart cut from the cadaver could be exhibitionistic (is the dissector proud of his skills?) or intimate (does he wish to share his experience?). It alerts us to a possible relationship between the poet and one of the *white-smocked boys* (5). *He* (11) may explain the use of the personal pronoun *his* in line 6 which at first reading does not relate to anybody in particular. Is her privileged access to a restricted area courtesy of a young male student? Plath seems at pains to keep her distance from what is happening. Coolly she likens the cadavers to *burnt turkey* (2) and *rubble* (8), bits and pieces of uneaten left-overs and rubbish held together with string. But the mood changes when she notices babies in specimen jars. The *moon* (10) image suggests the bleached colour and curved shape of the tiny foetuses suspended in formaldehyde and her unusual grammatical use of *moon* (10) as an active verb like *glow* (10), conveys a sense of softly radiating life.

The second stanza moves abruptly to a description of Brueghel's painting *The Triumph of War*, which hangs in the Prado gallery in Madrid. Only the lovers, protected by their exclusive joy in each other, are immune to the visible presence of death. Again the one-line space indicates a pause between the poet's description of the scene and her reaction to it. This time her response is more reflective and the verb *spares* (21) shows more clearly where her sympathy lies. Does it force you to reconsider the first stanza? Does it alter your feelings about what happens in the dissecting room?

6   **cadaver**   medical term for a corpse.
11   **cut-out**   the heart is literally cut out but the sense of a paper heart, a 'cut-out', is also present. Do you find the gesture romantic or does it shock you?
12   **Brueghel's panorama**   Peter Brueghel was a sixteenth century Flemish painter.
13   **carrion**   dead and rotting flesh, eaten by the birds of prey who traditionally hovered over battlefields and scenes of carnage.
21   **stalled**   halted. In what sense can *paint* halt the *desolation?*

Metaphors

Like a 'What am I?' riddle in a child's nursery book the metaphors are a set of clues. Further clues lie in the number nine; nine lines of nine syllables mirror the months of pregnancy. The metaphors are an oddly assorted lot. It is part of their childish charm. Could their random, varied nature reflect the contradictory emotions women experience during pregnancy?

One way into the poem is to decide what feeling is suggested by each metaphor. Some are homely images radiating satisfaction, some are proudly fruitful, some ludicrous, but some seem grudging, suggesting regret, even resentment at her pregnant condition and loss of control. As she realizes the responsibility that lies ahead, the playful tone sobers down and the closing image is coolly ambiguous about her feelings.

Plath was not pregnant when she wrote the poem. Her first child would not be born until a year later. The title draws attention to the poem as an experiment in language and it can be seen as another of her early, consciously crafted pieces: the tight formal structure, the syllabic rhythm and the occasional half-rhymes *house/purse* (2,6) and *calf/off* (7,9).

 5 'A bun in the oven' is a colloquial expression for pregnancy.
 8 **green apples** what does this image suggest: stomach pains; food cravings; the apple Eve ate in the Garden of Eden?

The Colossus

The original Colossus was a huge statue, one of the seven wonders of the ancient world. Where is Plath's strange scene set? The poem mixes classical references *fluted bones . . . acanthine hair* (20), *cornucopia* (24), a *hill of black cypress* (19) and a *sky out of the Oresteia* (16) with modern domestic, cleaning materials *gluepots and pails of Lysol* (11). Silt and weeds choke the stone head yet barnyard sounds proceed from its lips. We seem to have come in on the last act of a mythical drama without sufficient information to make sense of it.

What is clear is the size of the broken statue – the skull-plates are *immense* (14); the eyes are like *tumuli* (15); the tongue is a *pillar* (27). The daughter who tends it is *an ant* (12) crawling over the *weedy acres* (13) of its brow. It dominates the landscape like a ruined idol and she serves it like a temple maiden, religiously and faithfully. Does she take pride and pleasure in her duty? Or do you sense resentment? Weariness? Consider the familiar way she talks to the statue. Is she trying to relieve her solitude or does her language sound like the muttered complaints of a tired housewife? Is she blaming the statue, and if so for what? There is a bond which she cannot break. Is it love or loss which holds her?

For some readers it is impossible to separate this poem from the facts of Plath's life. Her father never lost his German accent (the barnyard cackles?). His early death left her with unresolved, confused feelings of anger and anguish which surface in this poem and also in *Daddy* (p.51). Less biographical explanations of the poem include readings which centre on the images of classical ruin, interpreting it as a lament for the damage done to European cultures by the devastation of two World Wars. Yet another way of reading the poem concentrates upon the puzzle of the eccentric sounds which the statue makes although his throat is full of silt. Could it represent the difficulties Plath felt about developing her own poetic voice in a literary tradition dominated by the canon of male poets whom she admired and copied, even as she tried to free herself from their influence?

11   **Lysol**   the tradename for a domestic cleaning and disinfecting fluid.

15   **tumuli**   rounded earthed-up burial mounds.

16   **Oresteia**   the title of the trilogy of plays by the classical Greek writer Aeschylus which tell the tragedy of the royal house of Thebes. King Agamemnon, returning from the Trojan wars, was murdered by his wife Clytemnestra and her lover Aegisthus. In revenge Agamemnon's son Orestes, urged on by his sister Electra, murdered his mother and her lover and was pursued for the crime by the Furies.

18   **pithy**   wisely concise. The father appears to combine the intelligence, knowledge and experience of the Roman senate (*Forum*).

20   **fluted bones and acanthine hair**   *fluted* refers to the grooves carved on the classical columns which his huge bones resemble. His hair is carved in curls like acanthus leaves.

24   **cornucopia**   the classical horn of plenty, out of which spilled fruits and flowers. Do you feel that this cornucopia offers her sustinence or it is ironically empty?

28   **shadow**   is she 'worn to a *shadow*' by her unremitting, useless labour? Or could the image encapsulate the poem's central rela-

tionship, that of a child unable to escape from the parental *shadow?*

29-30   This is the first mention of a possible rescue and it only serves to intensify the sense of hopelessness. What effect is created by calling the stones *blank* (30)?

Mushrooms

Each line has five syllables, unstressed, short, unemphatic and yet how relentlessly they sweep on, like the meek, bland mushrooms inching their way into our attention. Sentences override line endings in the smoothly insidious forward momentum. The tone of the mushrooms' childish address (*Our toes, our noses* [4]) is intimate and confiding; short phrases, colloquial syntax and pronouns establish their apparently gentle personalities. They seem so harmless. How could anything *edible* (27), *Soft* (10), *meek* (26), *Earless and eyeless* (15) and *voiceless* (16) be other than vulnerable and weak?

But there is another side to their personalities. Shy, quiet, discreet, they are also tenacious and determined. Modest in their needs, *asking/ Little or nothing* (21-22), dieting on *water* (19) and *crumbs of shadow* (20), they have the power of numbers, stressed by repetition and exclamation, *So many of us!* (23-24). Is the final image comforting or menacing? And if you feel that the mushrooms are menacing, whom do they threaten?

32   The phrase is taken from the Beatitudes, Christ's Sermon on the Mount where he preached: *Blessed are the meek; for they shall inherit the earth* (Matthew 5,3).

You're

In a jaunty manner, somewhere between the playfulness of a nursery rhyme, the trickiness of a riddle and the admiring tone of the Cole Porter song, *Baby if I'm the bottom you're the top*, this poem heaps up metaphors to praise the child in the womb. It is similar to the riddling style of *Metaphors* (p.41) except that Plath has moved from *I'm* (1) to *You're.* What difference is there between the mother's point of view in *Metaphors* and the focus on the child in this poem?

At the beginning the metaphors convey a joyful sense of the baby's gravity-defying freedom of movement. Gradually the child's separate existence emerges. From being *my little loaf* (9) and *our travelled prawn* (12) the baby takes on its *own face* (18). One of the best ways into the poem is to ask what each metaphor adds to the picture of the unborn child.

3   **Gilled like a fish**   a reference to the fluid in which the embryo lives?

7-8   **Fourth/Of July to All Fool's Day**   the fourth of July is America's Independence Day and All Fool's Day is April the first. The time span indicates the nine months of pregnancy but can you think of further significances?

9-11   How does the point of view change here?

12   **Atlas**   in Greek mythology, the giant Atlas carried the world on his shoulders. He was depicted with a curved back, bent beneath the weight of the globe.

13   **Snug as a bud**   echoes the familiar saying, 'snug as a bug in a rug'. What difference does it make that 'bug' is changed to *bud* and that 'rug' becomes *at home*?

15   **creel**   an eel trap made of wickerwork.

Morning Song

Love (1), abstract and absolute, sets everything going. (You might ask whose love?) There is something delightfully practical and workman-like about the baby's arrival, immediately at home, taking *its place* (3) and stating its needs *clean* (15) and *clear* (18). Not so the parents who appear discomforted and bewildered. The child is a *New statue* (4). The adults stand *round blankly* (6) at a loss how to react. Their first instinct seems to be to distance themselves and the poet feels the baby belongs more to the *elements* (3) than to herself. Her fragility, her inse-curity is suggested by the image of a cloud effaced by the wind. *Effacement* (9) implies a loss of personality as well as a willing submis-sion to the demands of the baby. Could the baby be a *mirror* (8) of herself, of her own making, but one which makes her conscious of generations succeeding each other and of her own ultimate disappear-ance? Is that why the naked child *Shadows our safety* (6)?

The fourth stanza suggests a new mother's anxiety while the fifth stanza shows a natural and instinctive motherly response. What does a *Victorian nightgown* (14) suggest? Whatever uneasiness is present in stanzas two to four, the poem ends as it began on a note of certainty.

The *dull stars* (16) are swallowed by dawn and the *clear* (18) notes rise in a happy image which promises the joys of childhood.

4 **magnifying** Plath may be echoing the Magnificat which Mary sang when she first felt Christ move in her womb. It starts *My soul doth magnify the Lord.*

7 An ambiguous line which can be read as rejecting or accepting responsibility.

Tulips

A woman lies in hospital after an operation. Images of negation fill the poem, of blankness and of letting go. *I am nobody* (5). *I have lost myself* (18). For 30 years she has been *Stubbornly hanging on* (23) to her name and address. Now she has given her *name ... up to the nurses* (6). She likens her state to the dead and resents the way nurses are trying to involve her in life, even in the passive activity of watching. *Stupid pupil* (10) she complains, punning on the word to show her rejection of their efforts and her resentment against a part of her body which is betraying her desire for complete emptiness.

Into this *calm* (50), *white* (2) ward the tulips intrude with disturbing boldness. What personality does she give them? Childish? They are *too excitable* (1). Military? They are *explosions* (5). Dangerous? *too red* (36). She associates their colour, a direct contrast to the hospital white, with images of wounding, bleeding, and drowning to death. The tulips leap to life, increasingly aggressive in each succeeding stanza. They *breathe* (37); they have eyes whereas she has *no face* (48); they *eat* (49) her air; they evolve into *dangerous animals* (58).

The symmetry of the poem is remarkable. Cold parallels warmth, white contrasts with red, numbness with *sudden tongues* (41) and there are further pairings. Hospital routines dominate the first four stanzas whereas the tulips fill the final four. At the centre of the nine stanzas the woman lies at her most physically inert, nun-like, *utterly empty* (30). Does the poem's remote tone, in contrast with the personal voice of other poems, reflect the woman's semi-conscious state or the draining away of personality?

Sea and river images run through the poem. (Light references are another related cluster you might like to trace.) The nurses pass like *gulls* (12), her body is a *pebble* (15) in a river.Were you startled when she likened the smiles of her husband and child to *little smiling hooks* (21)? The metaphor acknowledges their pull, the *catch* (21) on her affections, but also the way she feels caught like a fish by their demands. The same weariness with carrying *baggage* (18) is conveyed in the *thirty-year-old cargo boat* comparison (22), in the air which *snags and eddies* (53) disturbing her sunken state and in the water which *went over my head* (27). At her most withdrawn she longs to eat peace like the dead *Shutting their mouths on it* (35). In the end she sips water *like the sea* (62). Is the warm salt taste a memory of past or promise of future health? Grammatically it is her own heart which *opens and closes* (60) in *sheer love of me* (61). It has become the *red blooms* (61) of the tulips. Are we to read this as meaning that her body will bring her back to life in spite of herself? Have the loving demands which the tulips symbolize broken through her *nun*-like, *pure* (28) indifference? It depends upon whether the tone seems one of reconciliation or denial at the end. Is health still as *far away* (63) as ever?

The Arrival of the Bee Box

Plath wrote a series of poems about bees. She called the first one, *The Beekeeper's Daughter*. As her father was an expert beekeeper, it is difficult not to feel his continuing influence; difficult but not impossible. You will have to make your own decisions about the degree to which biographical details are a help or a hindrance. One can approach the poem directly as a study in control, asking who controls whom? An almost obsessive concern with authority is apparent in Plath right up to her final poems. You could look back at *The Colossus* (p.41) and *Tulips* (p.45). Is there any gain in control or confidence here?

3   **coffin** were it not for the *din* (5) the bees might be dead. Where else in the poem does she recognize that she has the power of life or death over the bees?

13–15 The image of a dark, angry crowd, made more explicit when she likens it to a *Roman mob* (19), creates a sense that she feels overwhelmed by the bees. There is something repellent in the picture of shrunken African hands. Is she using the implied racism to convey her growing fear?

21   The noise of the bees, their *unintelligible syllables* (18), is now an ancient language. The bees are becoming more alien and of great antiquity.

24–25   Do you find the tone assertive or hesitant? (*can* [24] implies its opposite, 'cannot'.) Notice how uncertain her language is becoming, *I wonder* (26), *If* (28).

   29   **colonnades**   the flowers of the laburnum tree continue the Roman imagery.

   32   **funeral**   the protective veil of a beekeeper reminds us of her power. The bee box could still become a coffin.

35–36   Has she reached a firm decision? Does the promise of what she *will* (35) be and *will* (35)do cancel her earlier denials *I am not a Caesar* (22) *I am no source of honey* (33)?

The Applicant

The title suggests a person seeking a job and the opening question sounds like an interview, although the tone is aggressive. It is unclear who is being interviewed or for what post. Even the sex of the applicant seems indeterminate, and the oddity of the questions which the interviewer fires so rapidly do not make matters any less confusing. Why should being crippled, damaged or sexually inadequate be a necessary requirement? Is the person applying for aid? What is clear is the personality of the interviewer. The tone is forceful, the questions abrupt, the manner hectoring. No space is given to answers or interruptions. We witness the interview from one side only. Its effect on the applicant has to be deduced from hints; *Stop crying* (8). And perhaps from the accusations of *Empty* hand (10) and *empty* head (26)?

Is it any clearer what is being offered? A *hand* (10), a *suit* (20), a *living doll* (33)? They are presented in the over-hyped language of product advertising and marketing, *It is guaranteed* (15), *new stock* (18), *waterproof, shatterproof* (23). You will recognize other phrases which belong to the high-pressure patter of a salesman pushing his wares. What first alerts us to what is being offered – the insidious repetition of *marry it* (14,22,40), or the patronizing *sweetie* (28) as the interviewer summons the *living doll* (33) from the cupboard, or the list of female duties? Plath's anger at the subservience of women in marriage burns through the humour of the macabre incident she has created.

Although women are depersonalized by the pronoun *it*, the doll is supremely confident beside the inadequate, sadly-lacking (male?)

applicant. What do you make of the insistent question *Will you marry it?* (14,22,40)? Is it ironic? (Surely you could not marry something so doll-like!) Or is it a warning to women to be less docile; to refuse to serve men who are *Empty* (10) or become a *poultice* (37) for male insufficiency? Do you feel Plath is being fair? Does her humour deflate the issue?

You may have noticed a change in Plath's style in this and the previous poem. Her stanzas are still regular but the lines are becoming looser. The apprentice years are over. From now until the end she increasingly frees herself from inherited poetical forms and writes in a voice which is distinctly her own.

16   The line describes the action of closing the eyes of the dead.
18   **salt**   salt tears.
20   **suit**   has the gender of the gift changed? If the other gifts symbolize a potential wife what is the applicant being offered here? A way of life? A dress suit? Marriage?
28   **closet**   American word for a small dressing room.
30   **Naked**   she appears to accrue in monetary value as the years pass but there is a sexual implication in a naked *doll* (33) which may explain the exclamation *that* (29).
33   **doll**   American slang for an attractive young girl.
36   **It works**   the verb encompasses the functioning of a mechanical 'doll' and the list of duties which Plath feels a 'living' woman is expected to perform in marriage.

Daddy

It is difficult not to read these lines at full speed. The simple, repeating 'oo' rhyme and emphatic monosyllables sweep one along. Energy pours out as intense feeling, matched by violent vocabulary, loosening lines, images of extreme horror and a furious hatred towards both father and husband. At the same time there is gaity in the tone; the use of simple, childish language, fairy-tale references and sing-song, nursery-rhyme chanting.

It is tempting to relate Plath's late poems to the biographical facts of her life: her father's German accent *Ich,ich,ich, ich* (27), his profession *You stand at the blackboard, daddy* (51), his feet, diseased by diabetes *one grey toe / Big as a Frisco seal* (9–10), her marriage, *I said I do, I do* (67), her attempted suicides *I tried to die / And get ... back to you*

(58-59), and her separation from her husband, *If I've killed one man, I've killed two* (71). As with *Lady Lazarus* (p.54) this poem arouses fiercely contradictory feelings in readers. Irving Howe, in his essay 'The Plath Celebration: A Partial Dissent' called it *a revenge fantasy, feeding upon filial love-hatred.* Seamus Heaney wrote that it *rampages so permissively in the history of other people's sorrows that it simply overdraws its rights to our sympathy* (*The Government of Tongues*, p.165). Yet its appeal is notorious. It remains one of her most famous poems, praised for articulating twentieth century women's anger at their position in society.

The poem does not proceed logically but in image clusters. One group relates to the *black shoe* (2), and seems to symbolize the constraining, constricting influence of *Daddy* (6). Another cluster belongs to folk legend, the *black man* (55) and the *vampire* (72) and symbolizes her feelings about the husband or lover figure in the poem who bit her *heart in two* (56). The central cluster of images of dominance and suffering relate to the Nazi deportation and murder of Jews in the concentration camps of *Dachau, Auschwitz, Belsen* (33). There have been strong objections to her use of the Holocaust. *There is something monstrous, utterly disproportionate, when tangled emotions about one's father are deliberately compared with the historical fate of the European Jews.* (Irving Howe, 'The Plath Celebration: A Partial Dissent'.) Other critics argue that the obsession with the father-figure arises from love, that her anger is really an expression of grief and loss and that the closing line is ambivalent. Is she *through* (80) with him or *through* (80) her rage? Is it triumph or exhaustion she feels?

Title   What difference would it make if the poem was called 'Father'?
    1   Curt monosyllables create a determined voice but also a child-like quality. How does the personality of this speaker compare with the daughter figure in *The Colossus*? (p.41).
  2-5   **black shoe**   the feeling of constraint and constriction is softened by the child's voice *Achoo* (5) and the echo of the nursery-rhyme, *'There was an old woman who lived in a shoe'*.
   13   **Nauset**   on the coast of New England.
   15   **Ach, du**   the German word for 'you' sounds loving, expressing her early adoration, although later she calls the language *obscene* (30).
   23   **foot . . . root**   meanings extend to include origin and penis.

32 **Jew**   as the speaker begins to identify through her *gypsy ances-tress* (38) with the Jews under Hitler's regime, German begins to mean Nazi.

42 **Luftwaffe**   German Air Force.

45 **Panzer-man**   a German tank trooper.

53 **cleft**   traditionally the devil has cleft hooves instead of feet.

55 **black man**   the first of the figures (*vampire* [72] is another) drawn from fairy-tale and folk-lore.

62 **glue**   points forward to the *model* (64) of her husband. You might like to think about why she can use glue successfully in this poem compared to *The Colossus* (p.41).

65 **Meinkampf**   the book Hitler wrote to propagandize his views of racist supremacy.

Lady Lazarus

> The speaker is a woman who has the great and terrible gift of being reborn. The only trouble is she has to die first. She is the Phoenix, the libertarian spirit, what you will. She is also just a good, plain, very resourceful woman. (From *Collected Poems* by Sylvia Plath, notes by Ted Hughes, p.294)

Were you surprised by Plath's last sentence? Here is a woman who has been brought back from suicide for the third time and apparently treats it as something to show-off about. She is a performer, a theatrical spectacle, a *strip tease* (29) and she charges, *a very large charge* (61). She is proud of her expertise in dying. *I do it exceptionally well* (45). Her tone is gay and insouciant, her voice lively, colloquial and mocking, her manner challenging and triumphant. Whatever does Plath mean by calling her *plain* or *good*? We are presented with a bewildering, boastful, aggressive woman who enjoys her control over audiences and doctors.

Mockery is present even in the title. The raising of Lazarus is one of Christ's miracles. He lay for four days in his grave until Christ brought him back to life. The parallel with the failed suicides is obvious but adding the word *Lady* makes the title sound like Lady Luck.

This 'Lady' regards the *peanut-crunching crowd* (26) with contempt and the doctors with hostility, addressing them as *Herr* (65), equating them with Nazis, with the enemy and threatening to eat them. Again Plath draws on the Holocaust for images which shock, both in themselves, like the comparison of her skin to a lampshade or melting to a shriek, and because this was actually done in the extermination camps. You will have to decide for yourself how you feel about this poem and whether it is possible, or right, to forget that her next attempt at suicide was only a few months away, and successful.

10 **Peel off the napkin** bandages being removed. Perhaps a reference to Lazarus' winding sheets? Is there a religious sense in *napkin*, and *fine ... linen* (8–9) of a cloth being removed from a sacred object?

17 **The grave cave** the flesh has fallen from her face leaving her bone structure exposed so her sunken features *terrify* (12). Can you see how the image also links to the Lazarus story and perhaps to Christ's empty sepulchre?

25 **filaments** fine threads. Is she thinking about the intricate threads which make up her body, or the wire filaments of electric bulbs lighting up her performance?

29 **strip tease** a witty pun on unwrapping bandages and stripping in a show.

39–42 It is important not to see the poem as an autobiographical 'confessional' piece but these lines appear to draw on Plath's suicide attempt when she was 20-years-old. She hid in the cellar beneath her mother's house, took sleeping pills and lay unconscious during three days of a widespread police search. By chance her moans as she returned to consciousness were overheard by her brother.

62–64 Is she turning into a religious or popstar idol?

67 **opus** work, in the sense of a major piece or work of art. How is the image continued in the following lines?

71 **burn** the word gathers up the idea of melting gold to make the *gold baby* (69), merges it with her physical pain and angry emotions, and points forward to images of burning Jews in concentration camps and the phoenix rising from the fire.

76–78 Cakes of soap were given out under the pretence that Jews were entering shower rooms in the concentration camps. Gold was removed from them before death.

Balloons

At the end of 1962 Plath returned from Devon to live in London with her two young children, to a flat which the critic Alvarez called

> chaste [and] forlorn [and] bare: rush matting on the floor, a few books, bits of Victoriana and cloudy blue glass on the shelves. (A. Alvarez, *The Savage God*, p.26)

It was bitter cold, the worst winter for decades. She wrote *Balloons* six days before her suicide yet it gives no hint of her desperate condition. All her poems about children regard them as a blessing and this is no exception. The bare room is transformed by the brightly-coloured, animal-shaped balloons. The delight they bring to the flat mirrors and the joy she experiences in the child's naïve, comical perception of the world as *pink* (24) and probably edible, is clear. In the course of the poem the point of view shifts from adult to child, the balloons transmute from *soul-animals* (3) to *Globes of thin air* (14). What point is Plath making about the way we see things?

2   **Guileless**   innocent.
3   **soul-animals**   is there a sense of the balloons being soul-mates to the children? If so, the adjectives in the previous line apply to both.
16-19   The artifice of the peacock image introduces an exotic note into the domestic setting. The blessing seems to come from a more sophisticated, wondrous sphere.
28   **clear as water**   builds on the image of a child as a *fat jug* (27). Is there a link with the second line?
29-30   **A red/Shred**   the popped balloon creates a humorous ending. Has it also removed a film so that he sees the world *clear* (28) or does his innocent 'contemplation' show him as 'guileless' as the balloons? Does the shift from pink to red suggest a move from a childlike world to an adult one?

Edge

Written on the same day as *Balloons* (p.58), it is impossible not to connect this, her last poem, with her suicide six days later and wonder at its calm obsession with how a woman looks after death. *The woman* (1) is distanced as *She* (12), no longer the dramatic, personal 'I' who speaks intimately in *Lady Lazarus* (p.54) and *Daddy* (p.51). She is still, rigid, white, carved: a statue. The feeling is of composure, of satisfaction in an accomplished finality. You can trace through the poem the words which sustain the idea of the dead woman as a beautiful, classical statue. Do you find the children at her breast disturbing, or does the gentle image of a rose folding back into itself integrate them into the placid scene? The moon is accepting, indifferent. Only two moments intrude, perhaps uneasily, on the quiet. In the garden *odours bleed* (15) and the moon seems cold and cut off (deliberately?) by a kind of radio static.

1 **perfected**   the finality of this statement invites no disagreement.

4 **Greek necessity**   Greek fatalism. The phrase maintains the tone of calm assurance set in the opening line.

5 **scrolls ... toga**   the classical garment is carved in loops.

18 **hood of bone**   the moon's colour. What else might be conveyed by this image?

Poems by Elizabeth Jennings

The Climbers

A frequent feature of Elizabeth Jennings' poetry is the quest for knowledge, some objective truth or goodness and the attendant question 'How do we know this?' In *The Climbers* the poet examines the idea of a party of men climbing up to some cold, inhospitable peak. The first climber reaches his goal but has no sooner achieved his object than he feels disappointment and envies the climbers below him still toiling upwards.

The poem shows a feature which you will soon recognize in other works – Jennings' economy of expression. In her earlier poems we find her pruning her language to its essentials yet abandoning nothing of its richness of association. The poem raises the difficult idea of motivation, a problem which did not seem to trouble poets like Brontë. Jennings seems to be asking herself why when life is forever confounding and disappointing us, do we consent to go on living? From what strange store of hope and idealism do we ceaselessly draw the energy to climb upwards? Unlike Brontë who seems to embrace the spiritual dimension ecstatically, Jennings' spiritual ascent is slow and difficult, a lonely and self-conscious journey.

1   **without their careful women**   it is significant that the women are left at home. Why are they *dispossessed* (3) and why do they see their menfolk as children?

3-4   **The mountain moves/Away at every climb**   the line poses the idea that every object we pursue flies from us and becomes an illusion which of course raises the further question – is any object worth pursuing?

6   **constructs himself**   because our personal identities are so fragile each man needs to construct his own path, but it is like a rope suspended over a glacier, perilous and possibly meaningless to others, yet we are all linked together.

9   **to see it whole**   one motive for the climb was to see the landscape from above, grasping the mountain's complete identity.

10-11   These lines imply a rather Brontë-esque idea that the mind's landscape grows clearer when *sinews strain and all the muscles knot* (11).

12   **One at the peak is small**   it is not obvious from whose perspective we see the events in the poem. From below the climber looks small yet he has reached the summit first. All things are relative and thus confusing. Arriving at a great truth may be a lonely thing – perhaps wisely the women stayed at home. Was the climb only an empty gesture?

14   He cannot remember now why he embarked upon the climb. What might his motive have been?

Kings

This short poem has a simple but suggestive structure. Note the subtle use of half-rhyme and the pithy memorable statements characteristic of Jennings' early work.

Many of Jennings' poems describe the nature of religious worship, the desire to understand a spiritual perspective initially grasped through the imagination. The poet was born and bred a Roman Catholic therefore her earliest imaginings were conditioned by a rich and unified set of symbols and stories. This is not a simple pro-monarchy poem, instead it examines our attitude to all kinds of gods, kings and heroes.

1   **out of doors**   imprecise, lost to the imagination – possibly connotations of exile?

2   **depose**   force to abdicate, uncrown. One English king springs to mind – Edward VIII, who in 1936, because of his wish to marry a divorced woman, was forced to abdicate. The poem has perhaps acquired renewed impact in the light of recent royal events.

3   **exile symbols**   kings are vivid symbols of a greater reality, of gods perhaps.
     take by force   the imagination is delicate, not to be handled roughly.

4-6   Individuality has taken the place of objects of corporate responsibility.

10   What are the *proper ends*?

12   Perhaps the crux of the poem. If we are unable to offer a simple act of reverence to earthly symbols of authority how can we respect ultimate authority?

Beyond Possession

This is a challenging poem grappling with how we perceive things and ourselves. It draws heavily on already highly charged symbolic structures – the river and the rose, which figure widely in art and literature. This early poem has something of the poet's youthful optimism, a vigour of expression which is not always evident in the later Jennings where sometimes the phrasing seems less tight. How would you describe the mood here? Would you say it is wistful, thoughtful, positive? Look carefully at the poem's title; what exactly is beyond possession?

4-5   **we write/ No emblems on the trees**   Nature is only itself and has no need of us to interpret its meaning. The poet may have Shakespeare's *As You Like It* in mind in which the hero Orlando writes love letters to Rosalind on the trees of the Forest of Arden.

5   **emblems**   as symbols or pictures imparting an idea greater than themselves. The rose is a complex symbol. It is obviously a symbol of the beauty of nature but it also has Christian overtones. The white or mystical rose has associations for Roman Catholics with the Virgin Mary. The red rose is an emblem of human passion – *My love is like a red, red, rose* (Robert Burns).

8 **sign our features** print our own lives upon it, relate to it personally.

15-16 This is a paradox. We look inward to private peace but must not always look for some reflection of ourselves. See *Mirrors* (p.66).

17-18 Is this the point of the poem? Jennings seems to search for the peace of the heart where *thought is free* (18). Perhaps we should imitate nature and be at peace with ourselves.

20 **shadow** the word has numerous figurative and applied meanings such as ghost, a constant attendant, a spy, an empty form, moral darkness or gloom, even death. Which, if any of these meanings apply here?

For a Child Born Dead

No attempt is made here to embroider an emotional subject. There is no hint of sentimentality. Compare it with Brontë's handling of a similar subject in *A Farewell to Alexandria* (p.6). Is it significant that Jennings has never married nor had children of her own? The poem shows a reverence for life but not to the extent that human life is everything. Perhaps the life of the spirit transcends the physical. Thus the child's rejection of our world makes it superior to us.

1-2 The child dies even before baptism; it seems like a rejection even of the church's blessing.

3 **a warm and noisy room** is this the womb or some kind of glorious pre-natal world? Why the word *room*?

12 The child was growing in the womb yet for what purpose when its end seems futile? The phrasing echoes a line from Thomas Hardy's poem *To an Unborn Pauper Child*, a poem about a child born to the poverty of the workhouse which records the persistence of life – *must come and bide*. Jennings takes the opposite view.

14 At last the event has meaning – our world is not good enough for the child.

Mirrors

Love is a subtle and complex theme in Jennings' poetry and is not restricted to sexual love.

This poem is perhaps about an instant attraction. The poet appears to fall in love with someone at a party, someone who seems familiar but only perhaps because he is a reflection of herself – a mirror image. Is such love, *as all self-love* (7), only an illusion? There may be a deeper idea involved and one the poet considers elsewhere. When we fall in love we may be admiring our own enhanced image, but such love, euphoric and powerful as it is, really belongs to *fair-grounds* (8) not life.

Again the poet is drawing on a depth of ordered symbolism. There are countless myths and legends involving mirrors. The most appropriate reference here is to the myth of Narcissus, a beautiful youth who fell in love with his own reflection in a fountain where he finally drowned thus forsaking the true love of Echo who pined away with grief until she became only a wandering voice. Narcissism, a psychological condition, describes the state of excessive self-admiration. Notice how other poets like Plath and Duffy refer to mirrors in their poems. (See Approaches p.228.)

1–3   What atmosphere is evoked? Does the word *talk* (3) have any particular significance? And why should it rise *to the ceiling* (3)? Is the conversation serious or just chit-chat?

5   **When at last you came**   there is a sense in which the speaker had summoned the other person to her. What does *something hoped for* imply? A love-affair perhaps?

9   **halls of mirrors**   one obvious hall of mirrors is in a fairground; this distorts our bodies and makes us laugh at our own absurdities.

11–12   Perhaps true love is blind to the imperfections shown up by a mirror.

In the Night

This is the first of a group of poems about the night sky (see also *The Diamond Cutter*, p.72 and *Remembering Fireworks*, p.74) a theme important to many of the poets in this collection. Like them, Jennings moves from starscapes (looking) to mindscapes (reflecting). Here the poet wonders what it is in the mind's eye which sees constellations in straight lines. The heavens symbolize something the poet is yearning for but at the end she finds them intangible and unobtainable rather as in *Beyond Possession* (p.64). She postpones the idea, turns away and sleeps. Compare this poem with Brontë's *The Prisoner* (p.19) and *The Night-Wind* (p.9). Does Jennings, like Brontë, appear to be someone who finds relationships difficult? It might be useful to refer to *Legacies and Language* (p.75) and find out more about the background and influences in her life.

1   **gape**   watch, but with an intrusive sense as though the watcher is an outsider, someone left out of an exciting experience.

11   **my mind is a room**   see the use of the word *room* in Notes to line 3 of *For a Child Born Dead* (p.175).

12   **scale**   climb. Is the idea of the mind something which outstrips the senses?

16-17   **thoughts about it divide/ Me from my object**   a difficult idea but one central to the poet and indeed all modern thinkers. (See Notes to *Thinking of Descartes*, p.184 for a wider discussion of this idea.)

Choices

Jennings often speaks to us as she would a close friend and yet she seems a shy, private person who does not tell us all. This poem may describe something about her motives for remaining unmarried, though we must not presume that this poem is a purely personal statement.

The speaker stands in the twilight outside the house. The group within would seem to be the stereotyped 'happy family' – perhaps a married couple with two children. We are not told why the speaker is visiting the house nor if indeed she finally enters it. The scene within, unlike the cold exterior, is one of domestic harmony. Bathed in lamplight it seems warm and secure. As in the previous poem the speaker is essentially an onlooker. Yet she tells us she has deliberately chosen this option though *Clothed in confusion* (12). You will need to decide who is the one who *looks out* (15). It may be someone with whom the speaker once shared a close bond, a need which still exists for both of them. Notice how the person within seems alert, pushing back his chair eagerly, opening a window. Why should he be so anxious to make the visitor welcome?

It is important not to see this poem merely at a prosaic level, that is only about disappointed love, for it is also about desire and values both private and mutual and how they may conflict with accepted social conventions. It may tell as something about the rôle of the 'outsider' in society.

3-4   Is there a hint of doubt or confusion here?

5   **shadow**   see Note to line 20 of *Beyond Possession*, (p.175).

6   **the cared-for lawn**   this hints at an orderliness which conflicts starkly with the speaker's *confusion* (12).

8   **A dog barks**   perhaps emphasizing that the speaker is an intruder.

9   **Comfort ... safety**   perhaps the major motives of marriage? These may not be enough for the speaker.

15   **windows**   notice other poets in this collection who have been concerned with opening or looking through windows – Brontë in *Stars* (p.17) and *The Night-Wind* (p.9) and Dickinson's *'I heard a Fly buzz – when I died'* (stanza 4, p.29).

Fountain

After winning the Somerset Maugham prize in 1955 Jennings was able to travel extensively in Greece and Italy. Spending three months in Rome, the experience changed her life and she wrote numerous poems. We sense here someone turning to nature and art as a kind of solace, perhaps for disappointing personal relationships.

The poet describes an elegant fountain in one of Rome's piazzas. This is probably Bernini's Fountain of the Four Rivers (1648-51) in the Piazza Navona (see Jennings' comment on Bernini in *Legacies and Language*, p.75). We first experience the fountain by its sound, heard in an adjacent narrow street, then as we enter the sunlit piazza its full beauty strikes us. As the poet gazes at it she marvels at that strange reconciliation of opposites – movement and stillness, light with shadow – which seems present in falling water. Almost always Jennings' appreciation of beauty is accompanied by a sense of loss – noticeable particularly in the last five lines – of nostalgia for something which has departed, glimpsed perhaps in childhood but never fully recovered. The prose-like form of the poem beautifully reflects the contemplative mood.

4   **window**   the word usually has connotations of soul or imagination.

5   **elemental**   a primary force, one of the four elements of earth, air, fire and water.

10   As the tides are ruled by the moon's influence.

14-15 **never/See the same tumult twice** the perpetual flux of water. Jennings echoes the Greek philosopher Heraclitus (500 BC) who maintained that everything is in a state of change. He was known as *the weeping philosopher* (*Oxford English Dictionary*) – an appropriate commentator on the concept of a fountain.

18 The fountain is surrounded by classical figures which seem to come alive in the shimmering light, the freshness of the air and the energy of the water. Their *bowing*, echoed in their *elegance* (23) seems in reverence to some water-god.

23 **taming** the artist has restrained some wild element, made it 'flower' and created *utter calm* (26). You could say that this is what the poet has achieved here.

27-28 The fountain restores the onlooker to a primary sense of child-like wonder.

My Grandmother

Probably the poet's best known work. It is a sad poem because it records how, as a child, Jennings was afraid of her grandmother who could not communicate the love and warmth which she needed. Her grandmother found a kind of substitute love in the polished objects of her antique shop but when age caused her to move to *one long narrow room* (14) – perhaps a hint of the grave – her treasured possessions merely looked out of place, reminding her how she had sacrificed love for those lifeless objects.

1 **it kept her** she was dependent on the shop to give her life structure and purpose.

2 **Apostle spoons** silver spoons – often given as presents at christenings – bearing the heads of the 12 Apostles on their handles.
Bristol glass antique glass made in Bristol in the Eighteenth century.

6 Jennings' grandmother seemed to polish away relationships. Perhaps human love, unlike antiques, does not remain in place, clean and tidy or beautiful, but is subject to change, often painful and unpredictable.The only love she gained, or wanted, was self-reflected. (See *Mirrors*, p.66.)

16 **shadows** see *Beyond Possession* (p.64) and *Choices* (p.68).

23 **no finger-marks were there** this refers us back to the idea of polishing in stanzas 1 and 3. Because no one ever used the furni-

ture it had no purpose except to gratify her sense of possession. The objects became both absurd and sad. Another meaning is that Jennings' grandmother is no longer able to leave her finger marks.

24 This is an ominous line. No amount of polishing can keep death – or any other painful experience – at bay. The dust will fall for ever and even her grandmother will not prevent it settling.

World I Have Not Made

A reflective poem in a prose-like form dealing with the mystery of existing in *a world I have not created* (16) and can therefore neither control nor understand. Jennings considers how it might have been if she had been able to create herself and her own world. Would it have been a happier place? It might have been more limited but perhaps it would have been more comfortable, like choosing ones own 'furniture' (see *My Grandmother*, p.70). Yet the idea seems impossible. Nature, difficult relationships, suffering, thinking, these will always remain; things which even *free faith* (14) cannot reconcile. The poem ends on a note of tension. Ideas seem insubstantial, shadowy; and beneath is always the abyss.

6 **Plato** (428–348 BC) Athenean philosopher and pupil of Socrates. Jennings refers to the Platonic doctrine that all physical forms are merely 'shadows' of eternal ideas.

14 **outlooking boundaries** not limited to the merely material world.

17–18 **There is a sweetness/in willing surrender** does the poet suggest that it is easier to give up trying to understand? Truth seems too immense to grasp.

21 **credo** 'I believe' – a creed or statement of belief.

24 The beast is reconciled with its true self, a state seemingly impossible for human beings. Can the *taut mind* (26) be at one with itself?

The Diamond Cutter

It is useful to compare this poem with *The Climbers* (p.62) and to note a familiar comparison of opposites *the white peak* (4), *the sun* (5). Like Brontë, Jennings seems interested in reconciling opposing forces, light with darkness, cold with heat. The task of the diamond cutter is to cut the facets of each gem so that it reflects an individual beauty and colour. Built around a series of couplets employing half-rhyme and internal rhyme, the poem has a more formal shape in tune with its theme. (See Approaches p.235, for evidence of Jennings' technical versatility.)

4 Why should cutting a gem-stone be like scaling a mountain peak?

8 **shun** reject. This seems odd, after all can a diamond have too much brilliance? Consider how physical light and spiritual light may be connected. In one of her poems Jennings contemplates candlelight, relating it to her own mind and spirit *in a dazzling dark my spirit stirred* (*A World of Light*, [12]). In which other poets' work in this collection do we come across this word *dazzle*?

Greek Statues

This is one of the poems Jennings wrote on her travels in Greece and Italy, and which, like her Roman poems, marks the release of a new energy. The poem seeks to understand the effect that ancient art has upon us. One of the most famous poems in English literature is *Ode on a Grecian Urn* by the Romantic poet John Keats. You might like to read Keats' poem and compare it with *Greek Statues* (p.72). Jennings, like Keats, is considering the nature of what the gods meant in ancient Greece, as well as the themes of time, art and beauty. The poet feels compelled to caress these figures, finding a calmness in their silent, dignified surrender to time. Note the way she contrasts unchanging things like *stone* (13), *Bronze* (11), *metal* (12), with human and impermanent substances *flanks* (9), *arms* (9), *eyes* (17), *flesh* (13). She feels chastened by *their large audacious gestures* (4). The figures do not seem part of a more human landscape *precious with grapes and olives* (18).

4 **audacious** dramatic, exaggerated – contrasting with *stillness* (2) and *surrender* (2).

5 **Remonstrance** protest.

12 **Gods into silent metal** the gods imply energy, power, even cruelty, yet here they are stilled into something silent. Just as the statue's eyes are *blind* (17), unseeing, the gods seem 'blind' to human suffering.

14 **Incarnations** the coming together of the spiritual with the

physical. The Incarnation is the embodiment of Christ as a divine being in the body of an earthly man. The Incarnation is of fundamental importance as a tenet of Roman Catholic belief.

The Interrogator

During a prolonged period of depression Jennings spent some time in a psychiatric hospital where she wrote poems on the themes of pain, death and despair. No collection of her work can do justice to her courage as an aritst without representing this darker side of her experience. The human mind has a frighteningly tenuous hold on reality. Life shrinks at these times

To what is suffering and small
The huge philosophies depart
(VI *Hospital*, 20–21)

The Interrogator examines her relationship with a psychiatrist. His clinical certainties contrast with her own uncertain but more feeling and complex understanding of life – an understanding which also recognizes its spiritual dignity. The poem reads like a verbal battle in which the narrator is finally so exasperated that she is ready to commit some violent assault upon the questioner. It is a battle which she knows from the beginning that she cannot win. Note the short, dogmatic statements which punctuate the first lines of stanzas 1–4; these reflect the interrogator's arrogant tone and his way of closing down all real communication. This encircling of her human responses by his unfeeling automatic ones again shows Jennings' skill with form.

10   **why you disliked your father**   a basic doctrine of psychiatry is the idea that mental illness stems from parental conflict – a view which in this case the poet finds unacceptable. You might however, like to look at her attitude to her father in *The World We Made* (p.79). For an interesting comparison see also Plath's *Daddy* (p.51).

24   This line describes the smug self-righteousness of the man. In stanza 4 we learn that he can *always find words* (13) yet having provoked the patient to lose her temper, he is pleased to remain silent.

Remembering Fireworks

As in *The Diamond Cutter* (p.72) and *In the Night* (p.67) the poet employs a familiar association of images. Watching fireworks is a commonplace experience yet Jennings uses it as a vehicle to explore a higher awareness of spirituality. You need to reflect on why fireworks, in themselves delightful, joyous things, should evoke feelings of nostalgia and things *surrendered* (15), *absence* (8), *emptiness* (9), something *known and lost* (8). Is it important that the poem is set in the past?

13 **'Yes, like that, like that.'** you need to consider what in this emphatic statement the poet is affirming. One explanation might be 'Oh! if only life could be like this!' Or she might be thinking about the actual problem of crafting a poem, *fumbling/For words* (10–11).

15 **We search for a sign** could this mean evidence of God? Perhaps it is an ironical jibe at the star that signalled the coming of the Messiah? Compare with Duffy's reference to Mary's anxious questioning of the heavens in *The Virgin Punishing the Infant* (p.94).

Legacies and Language

This is a useful poem to introduce Jennings' poetry for it describes her background from her birth in Lincolnshire with its flat landscape, her education at Oxford and the profound effect of Italy on her religious belief (see Notes to *Fountain* p.178). Her poetry seems like a dance of different cultures. (See Approaches pp.219–220 and p.232.)

11 **legacies ... inheritance** is there any reason why the poet should choose these legal terms?

21 **Renaissance** a period of European history between the medieval times and the modern beginning in Italy in the early Fifteenth century. The word means re-birth or revival (of classical learning) and is therefore appropriate to the poet's own cultural history. The movement questioned medieval dogma just as Jennings sometimes questioned the Catholic faith. (See Note to line 28 on p.184.)

23 **Raphael** Italian painter (1483-1529) especially noted for his supreme technical qualities.
Vatican the spiritual heart of Roman Catholicism in the centre of Rome; the palatial residence of the Pope. It is so called

because it stands on Vaticanus Mons (Vatican Hill) – the head-quarters of ancient Roman soothsayers and oracles.

25 **Pantheon** a circular Roman temple. It was dedicated to all the gods but became a Christian church in the Seventh century AD. Raphael is buried there.

28 **Had to argue with flesh and blood** the child's simple faith had to do battle with the realities of human suffering – a constant theme.

29 **catacombs** burial chambers beneath Rome. Their develop-ment in the Third and Fourth centuries AD was due to the spread of Christianity. Christians held meetings here and hid from persecution. Jennings may choose the word because her own faith sometimes flees underground during periods of depression and doubt.

31 **Baroque** sixteenth and seventeeth century art, a florid, deco-rative style associated in particular with Bernini.

32 **Bernini** Gianlorenzo Bernini (1598-1680) a sculptor and painter who was responsible for many of the great Roman build-ings including the great Piazza of St Peter.

Thinking of Descartes

Here the poet considers the seventeenth century French philosopher René Descartes whose work she admired and whose courage and patience as a thinker led to the famous dictum *cogito ergo sum* – *I think therefore I am* (23). The idea is also raised in *In the Night* (p.67). Descartes' view was that we cannot accept as true anything about which we can have the slightest doubt and he tried to empty his mind of all such beliefs. The point at which his doubt stopped was the reflection that he himself was engaged in thinking. Jennings compares this special kind of mental energy which can pierce the *dazzle* (19) with the poet's, which is more concerned with feelings; and often with doubt. You need to think about the ways in which poets and artists may be *partial* (35). Note that the poem ends on the most positive of all words – *Yes* (48). Think why the poem focuses on this word.

3 **Aristotle** Greek philosopher and pupil of Plato (384–322 BC).

4 **Thomas Aquinas** great medieval thinker and the funda-mental philosopher of the Catholic faith.

5-6 **'How much,/If anything, can our minds know?'** a question which is always central to Jennings' poetry. Descartes conceived the world as divided between observer and observed. What he called *me* (intellect or soul) and *body* (extension). (Descartes, *Discourse on the Method*, 1637.)

13   **On those pure peaks**   a cold, yet ideal world of concepts.

15-16   A central concern of Descartes was how can we know God exists? He argued that this idea is unique and the mere fact that we have this idea proves that there really *is* something corresponding to it; that is, there really *is* a God.

19   **dazzle**   you may recognize this as a favourite word of Brontë's. How does Jennings' use of it compare? One meaning here may be the idea that ultimate truth is too difficult for human comprehension, dark with excess of light. Descartes discovered the *Cogito* (27) while meditating upon a candle flame.

32   **Swarms**   think of a reason why the poet uses this word (See also Plath's *The Arrival of the Bee Box*, p.48). Does it mean confusion, pressure?

The World We Made

The dawning of self-consciousness is for the poet a sad moment. Childish imagination withdraws and the disordered world of adult responsibilities and acquired values takes its place. The poem is not just about lost childhood fantasy but about the history of the world. We sense a contrast between the pagan civilizations which worshipped the sun and the Christian one which looks inward and is stricken by conscience. It is not made clear to which world the poet is drawn. The poem ends on a sad note and words like *meaningless* (26), *troubled* (27), *distress* (28), *spoilt* (31), *cold* (32) suggest regret and longing for a simpler past.

1   Childhood may be a time when the self is not fully present. The child lives almost 'outside' himself.

3   **We did everything totally**   with full commitment, in contrast with the doubts and compromises of adulthood.

9   **cochineal**   a bright crimson dye. Is it significant that this is also the colour of blood? Which lines in the poem refer to uncontrolled emotions and violence?

23   **dervish**   associated with an Arabian tribe, the Dervishes noted for their wild, whirling dances in which they achieved 'out of the body' experiences. It also suggests something pagan.

27–28   **'You are/Christians, you know.'**   the statement falls like a cold judgement on the children's fervour, spoiling their happiness for ever.

42–43   **imagination was /Something to do with art and poetry**   imagination had changed from being something spontaneous to an acquired craft.

46   **colouring essence**   compare this bland abstract description with the earlier *The god we worshipped we named Cochineal* (13). (See Approaches p.234.)

51   Do you agree that teenagers are conscious of *little but themselves* and are no longer *free/To dream* (51–52)?

It Is Not True?

It is useful to compare Brontë's confident view of death and hope of eternity with this modern, uncertain view. Notice how the statements are often negative, imprecise: *where and how* (19), *somehow* (28), *It can't be so* (2), *I think we were in part* (25). The poet can only *hint at lastings* (34). Death is referred to as something slightly taboo which happens not to us but strangers *when we were not there* (12). It is an event only confronted directly when someone we love is taken ill and dies. Love as an eternal power is both questioned and feared. Even works of art may be transient *We think they'll last* (27). Unlike Brontë's poem *Death* (p.15) which challenges death directly and ends on a triumphant note, the poet here is submissive and apprehensive *O love I am afraid of this as well* (36). In what other poems have we seen Jennings *afraid* of love?

Still Life

Jennings was obviously much influenced by the Impressionist painters of the late Nineteenth and early Twentieth centuries whose use of light and shade seemed like *creating the world again* (3) (a line from her poem *Bonnard*). The title of this poem hints at the central paradox of art, to capture the movement of life in some permanent form – still / moving. Painters like Cézanne and Van Gogh take a simple object like a chair but show its mystical presence. The poet tells us that this is quite unlike pop art which gives only a photographic likeness. Art and life are not the same – style transforms the merely physical form and can 'move' us *almost to tears* (30).

4 **Cézanne's *Apples*** Paul Cézanne (1839–1906) a French painter associated with the Impressionists whose work led to the development of Cubism or the simplification of forms into abstract shapes and colour. His painting *Apples* is perhaps his most famous.

5 **Chardin** Jean-Baptiste Chardin (1699–1779) a painter of the French school thought to be master of the art of still life painting.

7 **Van Gogh** (1853–1890) a Dutch painter. His paintings exhibit a new approach to light and harmony and vibrant energy. He suffered long periods of insanity, spending much of his life in asylums and finally shot himself.

10–11 **Pop artists/or Op ones** the poet refers to modern painters who present an everyday object and make no artistic comment. Jennings uses the word *Op* (11) as a sarcastic suggestion that perhaps such work is practised deception.

Poems by Carol Ann Duffy

Head of English

This poem is an appropriate one with which to begin our study of Duffy, where she considers the rôle of a *real live poet* (2). The experience seems to have been unproductive for everyone. We see the event through the eyes of the Head of English whose dated views of the subject show us that for him/her only 'dead poets' are respectable.

2 Does this line convey a degree of recognition of the poet?

8 **assonance** a repetition of vowel sounds.

10 This line suggests that the school places high value on discipline. There is no sense of poems being enjoyed, only 'appreciated'; even whispering is *out of bounds*.

12 **we're paying forty pounds** the teacher is determined to get value for money. The fee seems to entitle the class to ask questions.

13 **English Second Language** these are children whose native language is not English.

15 **this person** the teacher seems reluctant to name the poet. Is it perhaps safer to have an anonymous poet when she is clearly not 'one of us'? See line 26. The word distances the poet from his/her audience.

17 This may be one of the reasons why the poet is resented.

18 **Kipling** Rudyard Kipling (1865-1936). Kipling's rhyming ballads and verses (obviously much admired by the teacher) are strongly associated with late Victorian nationalism and the Empire.

19 **the Muse** in Greek mythology Calliope is the muse of epic or heroic poetry and of poetic inspiration.

21 **winds of change** the phrase was used by the British prime minister Harold Macmillan to describe political changes throughout Africa in the 1960s. It has become associated with the waning of British imperialism and echoes the earlier reference to Kipling.

24 **something we don't know** the phrase implies a refusal to keep an open mind and the view that 'modern' poets can have nothing new to say.

25 **Well. Really** you need to think about the tone of these two words. Has the Head of English heard more than he/she expected or perhaps been offended or just bored?

27-30 The Head of English is keen now to get rid of the poet, a cursory leave-taking is transferred to Tracey. What do you think Tracey's views of the poet might be?

Standing Female Nude

Duffy compares here the stereotyped 'artistic' view of women with a 'real' woman. To the artist she is a relationship of shapes, volume, space, a group of related objects *Belly nipple arse* (2), an anatomical specimen, even a piece of flesh to be *hung/in great museums* (5-6). Instead of being diminished however, the woman seems to be untouched by the artist's need to control and categorize her. She has no particular respect for him even though he is said to be a genius. She laughs at his pretensions and his over-serious, bourgeois approach. He is just a *Little man* (19) who can only afford *Twelve francs* (28), not even the full price of her sexual favours. Note that the title consists of abstract terms which try to de-humanize the woman. Is this perhaps a comment on the way men look at women?

2-3 These lines emphasize the anatomical sense of the woman. In a sense the painter carves up her body on the canvas. (See Notes to lines 13–16 of A *Healthy Meal*, p.190.)

3 **he drains the colour from me** there is something of the vampire in the artist's gaze.

5-6 **hung/in great museums** again this has echoes of meat, perhaps hanging in an abattoir. What does this imply for art galleries? The theme of cooked and prepared meat is referred to frequently in Duffy's poetry, a theme she shares with the modern painter Francis Bacon.

24 **My smile confuses him** like the enigmatic smile of the Mona Lisa it distances her from the painter, mystifies and even deifies her. It also makes him think she wants him.

27 **he shows me proudly** like a child who 'proudly' shows its mother a painting done at school?

28 **Twelve francs and get my shawl** the pay-off and the brush off. Do you think the final statement *It does not look like me* makes a comment on how women see themselves? (See Approaches pp.226–229.) Or does she expect a realistic not an impressionistic likeness? How far would you say the poem is a statement about women's independence, even superiority over the male sex? Your view may depend on whether you are male or female.

A Healthy Meal

The poet registers here her revulsion for meat and brings to bear all her powers of wit and aggressive verbal agility to a powerful presentation of a scene in an expensive restaurant. Various dishes are described, but stripped of their culinary mystique, they acquire a macabre even surrealistic nature. The French words on the menu seek to disguise the horror of what the customers are consuming, the gruesome relics of slaughter. Does it also perhaps call up more dreadful images of concentration camps? Or even hell itself? Remember that Duffy is a Roman Catholic for whom the laws of fasting mean not partaking of meat for the soul's 'health'. What therefore does the word 'healthy' mean in this context?

1 **gourmet** someone who relishes and understands the art of cooking and perhaps eats to excess.

2 **tossed lightly in garlic** the idea of cow's dreams (brains?) prepared in this way is grotesque yet amusing.

green door   the green baize door dividing the kitchen from the dining room.

2-3   swish/of oxtails   again the idea has surrealistic nightmarish overtones. Do you consider her preoccupations vicious, outraged, ironic, resigned?

4   Duffy might be thinking of the stoop of holy water at the entrance of a Catholic church which also absolves guilt.

7   saffron   a yellow spice used for colouring rice.

9   language of tongues   here is a good example of what we might call Duffy's metaphysical wit. The tongues are dead yet they speak a language of silent contempt.

10   armagnac   a liqueur.

13-16   Duffy comments on the art of *charcuterie* (14) – the skill of cutting up joints of meat.

19   jowls   jaws.

20   The poem ends on a nauseating thought. The word *bowels* rhymes with *jowls* (19) drawing attention to the two stages of digestion.

Recognition

All the twentieth century poets in the collection are concerned with the way women conform or differ from those stereotypes which are often created by men. Duffy avoids looking at women in a heroic or legendary landscape like Boland (see *Anna Liffey*, p.122 and *Suburban Woman: a Detail*, p.106), preferring a purely domestic one. Here she presents us with a typical middle-aged woman shopping in a supermarket. She reveals classic menopausal symptoms *in a hot flush* (28) yet her day dreams define her as unique, truly 'herself' in contrast to the impoverished image revealed in the mirror. Most of the poem describes the dreary routine of buying groceries. At the check-out she realizes she has forgotten her purse and as she rushes out in confusion, she confronts her own image in a mirror and sees herself for a moment as a complete stranger.

The woman's life is seen as a series of broken images. The short, staccato sentences, sometimes only a single word, not only define her social class and her almost defeated view of herself, but tell us something about how women in general compartmentalize their lives. The world of *Quiche* (15) and *Kleenex* (25) seems to have no part in a romantic past where *A blond boy swung me up/in his arms* (15-16).

  2 **I've let myself go**   the first of a series of clichés. See how many
     other stale phrases you can find in the poem. What do these
     phrases tell us about the woman speaker?
 20 **creamy ladies**   models in the window. The woman has put on
     weight and compares herself unfavourably with these plastic
     shapes.
 22 **The waste**   what precisely do you think she refers to?
 24 Why should the shopgirl be *compasssionless*?
 29 **matron**   an elderly married woman.
31–32 Consider the implications of these last two lines. Why does she
     not recognize herself at first and why does she repeat the word
     sorry (32)? Remember that the poem is called *Recognition*.

The Dolphins

At the more obvious level this is a description of the dolphin's view of
existence as it explores the limited, hopeless world of the dolphi-
narium, longing for the freedom of its real home the ocean. At a
deeper level it may speak of the suffering of humanity as it struggles to
understand the relationship between infinite, spiritual desires and a
seemingly alien mortality. It combines both the concrete and abstract
and is a kind of metaphysical poem which speaks of Creation and
God. In reading this poem you will need to keep these two levels
balanced in your imagination; seeing how each illuminates the
other.

There is a beautifully simple articulation of profound thoughts
here. The poignancy and sadness of the poem lies in the way the
dolphin – like a human being – struggles to know the unknowable
and finally realizes that in such a world there are neither answers, nor
hope. Is there any reason why Duffy has chosen a dolphin as a suitable spokesman for mankind? You will need to ask yourself who is *the
other* in lines 4, 14 and 21? Is this perhaps the man who blows the
whistle in line 25 or some idealized form of the dolphin itself? Or
perhaps a companion dolphin?

  4 **The other has my shape**   could this mean that the dolphin, an
     intelligent creature, wishes to become like his master man?
     Perhaps this adds another layer of sadness to the poem.
  6 In what sense are the hoops and later the coloured ball and the
     plastic toy degrading to the dolphin? Why should performing

tricks for his master make him feel guilty? Does the master also feel guilty?

9　The repetition of the word *blessed*, echoed again in line 13, perfectly expresses the creature's aching sense of loss and man's cruelty. Perhaps the line also suggests mankind's fall from grace and God's displeasure. Man too has been expelled from Paradise. Can such a God be a loving one?

12　If man is *above* the dolphin, who is above man?

14　**will not deepen to dream in**　this is a complex and profound idea suggesting a number of meanings. The dolphin seems trapped between the lower world and the upper air which he only sees in brief glimpses. So, too, man is allowed only a glimpse of spiritual reality. In what part of ourselves do we dream?

16　**silver skin**　what other silver objects are there in the poem?

19　**The moon**　is this the *coloured ball* (17)?

19-20　The reference to *grooves* (19) and *Music* (20) may suggest the shining surface of a compact disc. In what sense are the dolphin's actions like a recording of music?

20　**Music of loss**　you may like to think of any other works of literature where animals are charmed by music or enslaved by man's need to control or dominate creatures he believes to be beneath him.

22　**There is no hope**　this is perhaps the saddest line in the poem. Do you think that it implies that for mankind there is also 'no hope'?

Ash Wednesday 1984

Duffy's Roman Catholic background emerges in this poem and it seems that like Jennings, her faith is not free from doubts. Catholicism is often associated in her imagination with pain, both mental and physical.The poem describes a day when as a child she attended an Ash Wednesday service and was *leathered up the road to Church* (12). It is about the intense feelings of childhood as well as religious indoctrination.

1　**St Austin's and Sacré Coeur**　two Catholic churches in Stafford.

2　**spanking wains**　this looks forward to being *leathered* (12). See also the poem *The Virgin Punishing the Infant* (p.94).

3 **a bigot's thumbprint dipped in burnt black palm** Ash Wednesday is the first day in Lent so called from the custom of marking the foreheads of penitents with the consecrated ash of palms remaining from the previous year's Palm Sunday service. A bigot is someone who has religious prejudices. The reference to *burnt black palm* (3) has a double meaning recalling Christian martyrs burnt at the stake for heresies and thumbprints used in the detection of crime and police records. You may like to consider the way in which guilt is part of the religious proceedings.

4 **Dead language** a poet uses language as a living organism which like souls and bodies cannot be restrained without deforming it. The reference here is to church Latin, a 'dead' language, yet in the poem *Prayer* (p.101) Duffy recalls Latin chanting as true prayer.

6-7 The children had to invent venial (pardonable) sins in the *dusty box* (7) – the confession box.

9 **slobbered** echoes *gobstoppers* (5) and suggests dribbling in a disgusting, possibly uncontrolled manner, akin to animals. But here it is applied to the rosary (a string of beads for the saying of 15 decades of aves, paternosters and glorias). Note again the many references to parts of the body as in *Standing Female Nude* (p.86).

11 Duffy was born in Glasgow in 1955. Many Scots came south in the 1950s seeking employment. Stafford was one of the 'new towns' of the period.

13-16 The verse describes the kind of religious indoctrination and psychological 'leathering', hated by the poet. St Stephen, the first Christian martyr, was stoned to death.

17-20 Forcing religion on the young makes the soul *sick* (17). The soul is not like an undergarment that can be easily washed clean, in its case by religious ritual.

18 **shamrocks** the national emblem of Ireland, also a symbol of the Trinity.

19 **transubstantiation** the Roman Catholic belief that at communion the wine and bread become the actual body and blood of Christ.
all my ass a crude phrase meaning foolish nonsense. The phrase in this context has other implications. Ass/arse refers again to the spanking of line 2 and some aspects of sexual perversion like flagellation associated with the scourging of

Christ and extreme forms of Catholicism.

20 **For Christ's sake** another colloquial phrase, yet having here a literal meaning. If you respect Christ do not force Mass on young, growing souls.

Words of Absolution

In *Ash Wednesday 1984* (p.90) Duffy deals with the indoctrination of the young. This poem is about the life-long effects of religion on an elderly woman about to die. She has known poverty and hardship. Now in a home for the elderly, she clings to her rosary as a last comfort. The poem is punctuated by the stock questions and answers of the Catholic faith. Old age is reached without certainty or contentment. And yet prayers, like music and poetry, because they are endlessly repeated, enshrine some strange and timeless beauty. You need to decide if there is one or a number of speakers in the poem.

2-3 **Who made you?/God made me** this echoes the Catechism which is a book that explains the principles of the Christian faith in the form of questions and answers.

3 **Pearl** one of her children who died in infancy?

4 **blacklisted** someone shunned or refused entry, a sinner, possibly the father of the child.

5 **patterns of your prayers** see *Prayer* (p.101).

7 **Original Sin** the Christian idea that all 'men' are born sinful. See Brontë's view of this idea, particularly in *A Farewell to Alexandria* (p.6).

9-10 This implies sexual prudery and guilt relating to sexual pleasure.

10 **Forgive me** *Forgive me Father for I have sinned.* These are the first words of the Confession.

11 **pass the parcel** death may be the parcel which we fear being left with when the music stops. The *parcel* may also be the old woman who is handed round the family. They fear as she gets older they will be burdened with her.

14 **Blessed art thou among women** this refers to the Virgin Mary. The words following *even if / we put you in a home* (14-15) imply that all women are not deemed worthy of blessings. Women are often deemed inferior by male Catholics. The family justify its rejection of her at the end of her life by stating that she is still blessed even if she is not loved.

16 **decades** stages in the rosary. It also implies things having extra value by the degree to which they have been used in the past. There is a sense of the woman being used, then passed between family members who do not want responsibility for her at the end of her life.

18 **Never a slack shilling** never a spare shilling. She fed and cared for her family even in times of hardship.

20 **Mary Wallace** an exclamation implying exasperation or annoyance; also a good Catholic woman?

21 **Chrism** the white cloth set by the minister on the head of the newly baptised. In Catholic belief it also applies to the shroud used by a child who dies within the month of baptism. See line 3.

22 A note of despair. How can you have an end of *nothing*?

23 **Sin of Sodom** homosexuality. Has one of the granchildren confessed this to her?

27 **Longanimity** a blending of longevity (long life) and magnanimity (generosity). Perhaps length of years implies the generosity of God.

29 The poem ends on a question. According to the Catholic faith, absolution from sin is a remission enacted by the priest almost as a judge acquits someone from a criminal charge. It follows confession and repentance. It seems that all the requisite conditions have been fulfilled yet the woman, at the age of 90, still clings to life. Has she received absolution?

Psychopath

This major and somewhat shocking poem presents a young man who is the archetypal male chauvinist. You will need to decide how realistic the portrayal is: whether he is a monster or merely the product of a disturbed childhood. The man is a fairground worker. Remember that his world is that of the bright, artificial lights and music of the fair which he brings to *dreary* (48) towns. The poem is set in the 1950s, a time of pop culture and rock and roll, a period when society was reacting against the drab days of post-war austerity.

1 **D.A.** a swept back hairstyle often worn by Teddy boys in the 1950s.
metal comb the stylized image of the pop idol combing his hair, a frequent pose of Elvis Presley's.

2 **Burton's** a shop selling men's off-the-peg suits.

3 **Jimmy Dean** a 1950's heart-throb, actor. He died young in a car crash in 1955 and has become an icon of the pop youth culture.

5 **crystal** crystal clear – slang of the time.

5–6 **crackling/in four petticoats** the word *crackling* (5) is a slang term for an attractive girl – a 'bit of crackling'. The reference here is also to the stiffened underskirts worn under the skirts of the period.

7 **wooden horse** one of the rides on a roundabout. It suggests also the wooden horse of the Trojan war, a conflict over the possession of Helen.

7–8 ***Johnny, Remember Me*** a popular song of the times.

10 **Brando** Marlon Brando, an American actor and another idol of 1950's culture.

12 **candyfloss** a pink sugary sweet. Remember the female 'look' of the 1950s, the era of Bridgit Bardot and Marilyn Monroe – the blond, fluffy, baby-doll image combining schoolgirl innocence and sexual allure.

15 **love myself** like the Greek god Narcissus who pined away for self-love, the psychopath breathes on the glass then wipes away his image. Is this an example of a personality which is falling to pieces?

20 **handrail to Venus** penis (rhyming slang).

23 **frenched it** French kiss.

24 **like they always do** a common male assumption that girls who say 'no' really mean 'yes'.

25–29 A flash-back to when the speaker was 12-years-old.

25 **Dirty Alice** a prostitute. Do you think her jeering at him was in part responsible for his later obsession with sex?

32–56 The rape and murder of the girl. Note the graphic description of details in 'close-up' – the dying goldfish, the defecating dog. Why should the poet choose these images? Note that just before the actual murder there is another flash-back to a childhood memory. The man recalls seeing through the kitchen window his mother having sexual intercourse with the rent collector, obviously as payment for rent. How do we know that the boy's father had agreed to this event?

43 **The sky slammed down on my school cap** do you think this traumatic event of seeing his mother in a degrading posture is part of his psychopathic personality?

44 **Lady, Sweetheart, Princess**   hackneyed words of endearment.

59 **dead ringer**   strong likeness.

60 **Ruth Ellis**   the last woman to be hanged in England. She shot and killed her lover outside a London pub. The man had treated her brutally but because she had crossed London in a taxi with the purpose of killing him, the murder was considered premeditated and thus carried a capital sentence. Ruth Ellis is now seen by some feminists as a martyr to male chauvinism.

62 **I could almost fly**   one of the sensations said to be symptomatic of schizophrenia.

64 **Awopbopaloobopalopbimbam**   a meaningless word but a popular refrain in songs of the 1950s. What point might Duffy be making about the language of pop songs?

The Virgin Punishing the Infant

Duffy seems to have been much influenced by the visual arts. Here she uses a painting by Max Ernst. In the picture the Virgin, also the speaker, is spanking the infant Christ who shows no emotion. It is Mary who is distressed; a complete reversal of traditional notions of the Madonna and Child. Duffy presents us with perhaps a more realistic view of the mother-child relationship. The poem makes us laugh but it has, like all Duffy's poetry, a deeply serious undertone. Again it challenges accepted views, making us think again about our prejudices and beliefs.

2 *I am God*   this arrogant statement comes as a frightening revelation. Joseph is driven into his workshop where he silently carves a wooden doll – something much safer than a real child.

3 **Pinocchio**   a wooden figure in an Italian children's story. Is there a link here between Joseph (*carving* [2] his wooden doll) and Gepetto, the lonely old man who makes Pinocchio because he wants a son of his own? Is Joseph making himself an alternative son?

6 *Gabriel? Gabriel?*   this refers to the Annunciation when Mary was told by the Archangel Gabriel that she would be the mother of God. Mary's anxious questioning implies that she would welcome a second interview in order to gain further advice on how to handle this precocious child.

11 Why do you think the other mothers believed Christ would

bring his mother sorrow? Why did they feel at first resentful and then superior?

15 **afterwards**   after what? See Note to line 16 below.

16 A suggestive final line. Such absence of emotion in the child might indicate stoic endurance (this could look forward to Christ's punishment at the hands of Pilate, which he accepts without complaint or reproach), silent protest or dumb insolence. Perhaps Mary cries because she finds that she is not so 'highly favoured', perhaps this is a picture of the Crucifixion or maybe Mary cries because it is not her place to punish her Lord.

Foreign

Duffy is interested in people who are outsiders, or who do not fit into a stereotype. The feeling of being foreign, and living in a large city without knowing the language, is an acute kind of loneliness. Language connects us with home. Without language the world breaks into fragments and is like a dream. Think of other characters in Duffy's poetry who seem to live in a shadow, even a nightmare world.

1–5 Where do you think this person lives?

12 Can you imagine what this name might be?

15 **coming to bits before your eyes**   the disintegration of society and even the falling apart of the human psyche are persistent themes in the poet's work. (See Notes to line 16 of *Psychopath*, p.196.)

Making Money

As a satire on our materialist society, this poem examines some meanings of the word 'money' – *I give my tongue over/to money* (2–3) and the poet finds over 50 different words to describe it. Perhaps the core of the poem is to be found in line 21: *Making a living is making a killing.* Duffy hides nothing of the stark reality of making money from prostitution, exploitation, the arms trade and other methods.

2 **tongue**   remember the poet's use of images to do with the mouth.

5 **Delhi**   the capital city of India and a centre of squalor and poverty.

Salaamat the *niyariwallah*   'greetings to the emptier of latrines'. The man squats by an open sewer.

7   **chapati**   piece of bread.

8   **pray**   a pun on the word 'prey'.

11   **pelf**   money dishonestly obtained, associated with the word 'pilfer'.

13   **snort**   slang for a rolled up paper for the inhaling of drugs.

14   **enema**   an injection of liquid into the rectum or the syringe used for the purpose. There is a pun on the word *enema* / enemy.

20   **Golden hullo**   money paid to bribe or introduce a customer.

22   **Jobbers and brokers**   people dealing in stocks and shares.

25   This line has an association with a painting by the Dutch seventeeth century painter Rembrandt entitled *Danaë and the Shower of Gold* which depicts the myth in which Zeus changed himself into a shower of gold in order to gain access to Danaë whom he seduced. Freudian psychology suggests that money can be a substitute for sex.

Letters from Deadmen

You might like to compare this poem with others in the anthology which look at death from 'inside' such as Plath's *Lady Lazarus* (p.54) and Dickinson's *'Because I could not stop for Death'* (p.30). It is a letter from an ordinary, working-class man, writing to his family, almost as if he is on a long holiday, or just 'away', and hoping they remember him. Is this one man writing on behalf of many *Deadmen*?

There is a contrast between the grave (dust, ash, loam, mulching skeletons, worms, snails) and the prosaic details of domestic life (wireless, photographs, stout, sandwiches) yet such information is conveyed with an equal tone of composure and resignation. This gives a disturbing feeling to the letter. An ordinary person is once again presented in an extraordinary light. Things are seen not from the perspective of time but eternity.

1   **femur**   thigh bone. Perhaps belonging to a relative.

4   **mulching**   sounds like 'munching' but means the act of putting compost or rotting leaves and twigs around the base of plants or trees.
       thrummed   a word combining 'drummed' and 'throbbed' meaning the beating of the heart.

6   **your sadness will be less**   to whom do you think the letter is addressed? Is it the one who brings violets – his wife or child?

7-12   He was an ordinary man. Which details fill out the picture of his earthly life?

16   ***they parted his garments***   words applied to Christ after the crucifixion (*Matthew*,27,35). Has the speaker's estate been carved up?

18   **Insurance men**   in working-class families insurance was often paid weekly to cover the funeral expenses. The insurance man often became a family friend who was invited to the funeral.

24-25   There is a twist of irony in these last two lines. The hackneyed ending to a letter *may/this find you as it leaves me* becomes 'you will also die soon' – a note of bitterness perhaps?

Small Female Skull

A disturbing poem which pushes back the limits of what is real as the poet metaphorically peels back the flesh from her own head to examine the skull beneath. We are not told exactly why the poet holds her head in her hands but like the woman in *Prayer* (p.101) we imagine that she feels miserable, desperate, having retired to the bathroom – *a white tiled room* (17) – in order to be alone. Which word in the poem gives us a clue as to the cause of this misery? Think of reasons why women cry alone.

In stanza three the thoughts become increasingly bizarre – *they will think I have lost my mind* (18). She gazes at herself in a mirror watching herself weep, losing control, even wallowing in self-pity. When she sees not a crying but a *grinning* (19) face as in the gaping mouth of a skull, she is arrested by the thought that there is something self-indulgent in all this. This is someone else crying. She seems like merely the ventriloquist for a speaking head or *a friend of mine* (20).

2   **ocarina**   a small egg-shaped wind instrument.

7   **It feels much lighter**   it is difficult to weigh one's own skull. The poet feels that hers could almost float upwards. What emotions might precipitate such a feeling?

11   **gottle of geer**   the words used by an amateur ventriloquist. The speaker feels a fake, a puppet operated by someone else.

19   Why should crying be a *joke*? Is it that expressions of laughing and crying can look very similar?

20   **a friend of mine**   herself?

The Grammar of Light

You might like to compare this poem with Brontë's *Stars* (p.17) or Dickinson's *'There's a certain Slant of light'* (p.25). Duffy seems to agree that light has a mystical quality; its subtle, changing effects constantly adjusting our way of looking at and understanding the landscape. People and objects we think we know are suddenly transfigured by an odd angle of light, revealing something strange, wonderful or frightening.

The title of this poem is interesting. Why 'grammar' of light? Is it that light is also a language for explaining things to us? Note that the metaphors here are deliberately odd, distorted sometimes, like strange tricks of light. There are many different types of light described and each articulates itself distinctly. Look carefully at the verbs used in each case.

1–2 Two lovers kissing?

10 **a wasteground weeps glass tears**   a striking image calling up thoughts of rain on broken glass.

18 **undressing in veils of mauve smoke**   an unusual image calling up perhaps the idea of the Jewish princess Salomé and the Dance of the Seven Veils (*Matthew*,14,6).

22 **slurs**   applied to words pronounced indistinctly, often due to the effects of drink (*wine* [21]?). The word rhymes with *blur* (23) and echoes *stuttering* (20). Note the use of internal rhyme and half rhyme *slur* (22), *blur* (23), *flare* (25). Like light and colour, language is infinitely subtle in its gradations.

25 **The way everything dies**   a negative conclusion; nothing is permanent.

Prayer

A simple poem expressed in almost monosyllabic words and almost exclusively nouns. Duffy seeks to express basic rhythms of ordinary objects and phrases – *a tree* (4), *a train* (8), *piano scales* (9) – a purely secular religion which consoles and uplifts both the non-believer and those whose hearts are hardened by life and are unable to pray.

2–3 The figure of a woman holding her head in her hands is one of those familiar, symbolic poses which we associate with grief or despair. It is Nature which revives her.

8 **Latin chanting** associated with the Catholic Mass. Perhaps the man, now without faith, attended a Catholic school. The train's sound reminds him of his lost childhood certainties.

14 These are the areas named in the shipping forecast. The familiar list of names sounds like a prayer, poem or song. Does it matter that only sailors may recognize where these places are? Remember that this is sometimes the last thing people listen to before sleep.

Poems by Eavan Boland

The Woman Changes her Skin

At the opening of the poem the narrator sounds weary. She applies her make-up in a dull repetitive manner, *How often* (1), *Again and again* (8), *the same* (14). As she emerges from her domestic routine into a creature of allure and entrapment her sexuality arises and the tone becomes sinister, hinting at danger which might be exciting or might be lethal. Can you identify the moment when she becomes a snake, a symbol of sin and sensuality, or is the transformation gradual? To whom or to what does *hood* (29) and *my tongue flickers* (36) refer? You might like to compare the transformation here with Keats' *Lamia*, where a wild, passionate serpent changes in writhing convulsions into a deceptively gentle and beautiful woman who seduces the hero to death.

29 **look** this imperative gives the woman a commanding presence. She gains authority as she sheds her skin.

Suburban Woman: a Detail

In her thirties Boland moved to the suburbs at the foothills of the Dublin mountains.

I led a life which would have been recognizable to any woman who had led it and to many others who had not. My days were arrayed with custom and necessity, acts so small their momentousness was visible to nobody but myself. Season by season I separated cotton

from wool and the bright digits of gloves from ankle socks. I drove
the car. I collected children from school. (*Object Lessons* pp.16-17)

Gradually she realized that the routines of her life were the same for
many women: repetitions which revealed deeper, mythic meanings.
She could find no voice for her feelings in contemporary Irish poetry
dominated, she felt, by male writers and by imagery which used
women as symbols, not as subjects in poetry. To give her voice poetic
authority she turned to classical mythology, merging the figure of a
suburban woman with the goddess Ceres.

The deceptively mundane, suburban setting of the opening shifts
abruptly to the Ceres and Persephone legend which is so potent in
Boland's verse. (See also *The Making of an Irish Goddess* [p.111] and
The Pomegranate [p.114].) In contrast to the clipped, crisp sound of
part I (all those hard consonants), touches of rhyme (*water/daughter*
[10,12] and *soon/rain* [13,14]), a more defined rhythm and short lines
help to establish the solemn tone of part II. Part III has a mysterious,
misty mood suggested by words which blur the clarity of part I. Its lines
are looser and its closing sibilants end the poem in a quiet whisper. In
the *lessening* (25) light the woman who was so *definite/to start with*
(23-24) becomes uncertain. Orderly control dissolves in undefined,
liberating but disturbing shapes which Boland calls elsewhere an *index
of coming loss* (*Object Lessons*, p.168).

How do you react to these changes in tone and where might they fit
with the changes in subject? There is tension in the poem between
winter and spring, between clarity and blur. What does the title indicate? Is the incident described in part III a trivial part a of woman's life
or does this detail contain the essence of the whole?

3   **gelded**   emasculated, trimmed.
8   **goddess**   Ceres, the Greek goddess of corn. The god of the
    Underworld, Pluto, fell in love with Ceres' young daughter
    Persephone and seized her while she was playing with her girl
    friends in the meadows. Grieving and distraught, Ceres sought
    for her lost daughter, finally discovering her in Hades. Pluto
    agreed to release her on condition that she had not eaten
    anything. Unfortunately Persephone had consumed six pome-
    granate seeds and for this he condemned her to return for six
    months of every year. During this time the Greeks believed that
    Ceres in her grief abandoned caring for Nature and let the world

lapse into winter. They saw spring as the time when she decked the natural world in joyful anticipation of her daughter's return.

29-30   The personified tree refers to the classical legend of Daphne who was metamorphosed into a laurel to save her from the passionate pursuit of Apollo.

Lace

Lace is fabric and language: a decorative flourish *at the wrist* (14) of an eighteenth century prince and the carefully fabricated words in which he phrases his well-turned conversation, his *crystal rhetoric* (20). The description of the fabric as a *baroque obligation* (13), something every *prince/in a petty court* (15-16) wore as a matter of course, is balanced by the labours of the lacemakers who lost their sight in making it. Similarly, the *thriftless phrases* (19) which the prince so casually *shakes out* (18) are paralleled by Boland's description of herself, struggling to find the right words. Male prerogative and women's work are opposed and each is brought into question, as are the issues of luxury and poverty, easy grace and costly labour, accomplished speech and striving for expression, *I am still /looking* (9-10).

The rhythm is based on a short line of two to four stresses, giving a ragged, lacy appearance to the edge of the poem. One line stands out visually because it consists of a single syllable. What effect does this have?

13   **baroque**   an ornate and heavily decorated fashion in art, architecture, music and dress which was fashionable in Europe from the Sixteenth to the Eighteenth centuries.

20   **rhetoric**   refined speech which uses elegant phrases to please or impress.

21-22   **bobbined knots/and bosses**   knots and bosses are formed in lace patterns by twisting the thread around bobbins. The phrase is grammatically linked to *crystal rhetoric* (20) and describes, as well as the fabric, the courteous and courtly language which the prince speaks.

The Achill Woman

This is the first poem in a sequence of 12 published in 1990 under the title *Outside History*. In these poems Boland explores the relationship between her own life and the history of Ireland, centering on the desperate period in the mid-Nineteenth century when over two million Irish died or emigrated in the terrible potato famines of the late 1840s. References to this *preventable tragedy* (*Object Lessons*, p.165) enter her poems obliquely from the angle of a twentieth century suburban woman recognizing what her life shares with the unrecorded, unvoiced, bitter sufferings of women who lived, bore children and died during the famines of the 'Hungry Forties'.

While she was a student Boland spent an Easter break alone at a friend's cottage in Achill, reading the poetry of the sixteenth century English lyric writers for her examinations. The cottage had no running water and the woman who features in the poem was the caretaker who carried water from the bottom of the hill each evening up to where Boland was staying. Achill, a small island off the west coast of Ireland, was one of the worst famine areas. The woman is unnamed. She is identified by a place, and the importance of that place in Irish history appears to be omitted from the poem. But is it?

6   **zinc-music**   the metal bucket is made of the alloy zinc.

9   **fluid sunset**   the setting sun is reflected in the stream as are the stars later the same evening.

18   **Court poets of the Silver Age**   sixteenth century lyric poets of the English Tudor period, men like Thomas Wyatt, Henry Howard, Earl of Surrey, and Walter Raleigh.

30–32   In contrast to the plain vocabulary of the rest of the poem, these lines echo the sophisticated language of the Tudor poets, most of whom lost their lives pursuing their ambitions. Wyatt was twice imprisoned in the Tower; Raleigh and Surrey were beheaded. Years later Boland explained her fascination with the lyrics of the Court poets *whose lines appear so elegant, so off-hand yet whose poems smell of the gallows* as arising from their being written *within sight of the gibbet. They breathe just free of the noose.* (*Object Lessons*, p.129)

Do you think Boland feels that her youthful lack of comprehension arises from the difficulty of understanding the nuances of Tudor language, or is it a failure to recognize the dangers of court life which lay behind the civilities of language? Or is she *chilled* (26) by a premonition of how resonant the Achill woman will become in her own writing?

The Making of an Irish Goddess

As her interest in history developed Boland went in search of her ancestors. They included a paternal great-grandfather who in the 1870s became master of the Clonmel Union, the dreaded workhouse. Visiting the site she imagined a woman arriving there, a woman like herself with two small children:

> her sufferings would have been terrible. . .She would have felt no hope at six a.m. when she rose; no hope at nine p.m. when she finished a day of carefully planned monotony. Yet she would also have seen the coming and going of the seasons. She also, like me, must have seen them in her children's faces. (*Object Lessons*, p.165)

In her earlier poems Boland had sensed a mythic pattern in the repeated details of her suburban life. The poems in *Outside History: a Sequence* recognize that her private life is *instructed by history. . . I gradually came to know at what price my seasons – my suburb – had been bought* (*Object Lessons*, p.174). Exploring the idea of what turns women into myths, this poem brings together Ceres and the defeated women of Irish history. Goddess or starving woman, they made the *same descent* (13) which the poet shares as she too searches for a child whose birth is marked on her body, *neither young now nor fertile* (15).

1   **Ceres**   see Note to line 8 of *Suburban Woman: a Detail*, p.203.
5   **arteries**   geologists call the thin layers of metal which appear in rock fissures and strata formed over time by shifts in the earth's surface, 'veins'. In keeping with the sense that Ceres inhabited an unchanging, *seasonless* (10) world before she lost Persephone, Boland may be using the more active phase in the blood's circulation to describe minerals in rock strata.
6   **diligence**   careful attention.
10   **unscarred**   the first mention of the image which will dominate the poem. After the loss of Persephone, the earth is marked and scarred by the seasons. Accident and childbirth leave *blemish*, *scar* (20) and *marks* (16) on the body of a woman. Notice how the *marks* (16) are both *wound* (31) and *inscription* (22). What might be the link?
13   **the same descent**   the act of seeking her daughter in the evening (35–42) is linked to Ceres' descent into the

Underworld. (See Note to line 8 of *Suburban Woman: a Detail*, p.203.)

23 **that agony:** the determiner 'that' links the phrase back to *that history* (12), the colon points forward to the description of the agony of the great potato famine (24–29).

31–2 The scar image culminates in the *wound* (31) which every woman who loses a child, even momentarily, feels *in the time we have* (32) . The poet needs both the scars in her own *flesh* (12) and a sense of *that history* (12) to share the experience of motherhood and loss which the myth symbolizes.

38 **sickle-shaped** what is the link with Ceres, goddess of the corn, in this image?

Outside History

The poem contrasts being outside history with becoming part of it. It balances the distant time when the stars were created with a closer historical period of suffering. Between these alternatives the poet must choose to be human or to be mortal, and she chooses to be human, to move out of myth and take part in the history of her country. The poem speaks to us in the first person. Who do you think is addressed by *you* (10)? And to whom besides herself does the poet refer when she writes *our pain* (5) and *we* (21)?

2 **inklings** slight suggestions or vague suspicion.

9–12 **human ... mortal** the first of these closely contrasting words suggests our capacity to feel, the second that an awareness of death adds to our understanding of what it means to be alive. Myths describe what is common in human experience while history records unique events.

16 **fields** the rotting harvest fields of the great famine. (See Notes to *The Achill Woman*, p.204.)

17 **roads** on which the starving and evicted Irish walked at the height of the famine as they wandered in search of food and work. The reference might also be to the roads built as part of the relief programmes set up in 1846 (see Note to lines 8–16 of *That the Science of Cartography is Limited*, p.209) on which they laboured and died.

The Pomegranate

Boland sees herself first as Persephone and then as Ceres as her own daughter takes on the Persephone role. Past, present and future intertwine as Boland reinterprets the myth of Ceres and Persephone. The stars were *blighted* (12) when she was a child (see Note to line 8 below). Now she is a mother they are *hidden* (25) and *veiled* (44).

  1   **The only legend**   the legend of Ceres. (See Note to line 8 of *Suburban Woman: a Detail*, p.203.)
  8   **a child in exile**   Boland refers to the period when her father became the Irish Ambassador in London. She was six years old.
35-36   Boland plays on the sound of the word pomegranate, dividing it between the French 'pomme' meaning apple, and the hard rock 'granite'.
50-54   Because Persephone ate six pomegranate seeds in Hades, she had to return to the underworld for six months each year. Boland's daughter is about to eat a fruit which, like Eve's apple, is an image of the knowledge of grief adulthood brings. What do you think the *gift* (49) is, and how does the act of giving it affect the poet? *And for me* (23) is not a question, yet the phrase is ambiguous. Does it refer backwards, recognizing that *winter* (20) is as inescapable for humans as it is for trees? Or does it refer forward to the mother's present dilemma?

The Parcel

The meticulous listing of each stage of wrapping a parcel before the convenience of jiffy bags, staples and Sellotape confers an importance that seems to grow until the act commemorates the passing of a whole era of knife grinders, *steamships* (37) and *out-dated trains* (37). It becomes an image of loss. Notice how the words associated with loss accumulate, *dying* (1), *distance* (9), *lost . . . missed* (33), *disappear* (35), *died* (36), *doomed* (37), *cracking* (41), *unravelling . . . illegible* (42). The abrupt phrases of the final lines have a surreal quality. Do you think they are describing parcels in the past or in the present? Or are they images hinting at more disturbing losses?

 14   **grindstone**   a machine with a whetstone for sharpening blades. Men used to call periodically at homes offering to resharpen domestic tools.

24   **terracotta**   the red blob of the sealing wax fastening down the string is compared to classical and Renaissance medals which were sometimes made from browny-red terracotta clay.

34   **burlap**   a coarse fabric, used for sacking, woven from jute or hemp.

That the Science of Cartography is Limited

This is the first poem in a sequence published in 1994 which Boland called *Writing in a Time of Violence*. In an interview with Jan Garden Castro, she said:

> I don't know that people can realize . . . the level of discomfort and anxiety and a small side-lining of grief that happens every day in a country like Ireland, where lives are torn apart and you also are a life with a small contribution to make.Where the witness is never big enough, where the eloquence is never great enough; where no rhetoric meets the situation; where no event saves those people. (*Tampa Review 10*, 1995)

In this poem Boland envisages a hanging wall map of Ireland which she can *take down* (17). It is shaded in different colours and the poem pays tribute to the knowledge and skill, the *Science*, needed to make such a map. The title however confronts and challenges us with the word *Limited*. In what way is this map limited? The poem answers the question by stating that *Science* is inadequate to record the human suffering which created the landscape it claims to document.

The poem's form is a regular four-line stanza although three times the fourth line is separated. Why do you think the poet wanted to make these particular lines stand out? Notice how long the sentences are, particularly the final one. Their full meaning is often delayed until the end and the negatives *not* (1), *never* (18), *nor* (21), *no* (27), *not* (28) help to hold back the sense of where they are going. The final line with its four hard monosyllables contrasts with the flowing rhythm of the rest of the poem, bringing it to a chilling close.

Title   **Cartography**   the art of map-making.

2–3   **balsam . . . cypresses**   species of trees. They summon up the sights and smells of the forest which a map cannot.

8–16   **famine road**   In the terrible winter of 1846–47 the British Government started a programme of 'poor relief' public works and by February of 1847 three quarters of a million starving Irish were employed building roads which often led nowhere and were never finished.

25 **the line** which should indicate the famine road in what is now woodland is personified and speaks in the voice of cartography and of the dead Irish. It *says* (25), *cries* (25), *gives* (26) and *finds* (27). The active, living voice contrasts with the flat denial of the last line.

The Dolls' Museum in Dublin

The dolls in the museum *Recall* (5) nineteenth century Dublin when Ireland was still part of the British Empire. Elegant officers and their mistresses *Promenade* (6) at leisure until war summons them back to barracks. In the *chilling* (32) *shadow* (32) of their carriages and in the *lilies* (18) in the churches lie reminders of the sacrifice they will be called upon to make. Light-hearted pleasures are juxtaposed with disfigured dolls; elegance with blemishes; fragility with strength; the past with the present; a moment in time with endurance. These suggest further pairings: sunlight and twilight; cold hands and warm; active life and museums; war and peace; rejoicing and sacrifice.

Boland also uses repetitions. The word *terrible* opens and closes the poem; *turning* is repeated in the line (28) where the officers are recalled from leave. *Shadow(s)* (32,33) and *twilight* (32,33) link nineteenth century Dublin to the present. The poem is held in a tight structure: stanzas of four lines and a rhyme scheme which, although it uses half rhyme rather than full rhyme, follows a strict 'abab' pattern. Is there a sense of something held tightly at bay? Of gaiety covering alarm? Of mannerly ritual disguising sacrifice?

1 **wounds** the word shocks, until the poem reveals it is a metaphor for the wear and tear on a doll in the museum. The resonances set up in the first line emerge later in the poem, linking the dolls' wounds with other sacrifices.

5 **Quadrille** a formal, patterned dance.

11 **College Green** in the centre of Dublin, near the River Liffey.

13 **Cradled and cleaned** the dolls are new and cherished by their owners. Is there an echo of how soldiers handle military weapons in the phrase?

17–20 The churches are dressed for Easter services with the Christian symbols of purity and sacrifice celebrating Christ's death on the cross and his Resurrection.

18 **surplices** white garments worn by priests and choristers.

24 **Shelbourne** a grand and famous Dublin Hotel.

41 **hostages** although this word is used metaphorically, it brings the sense of hostilities closer .

Inscriptions

With a sense of excitement the poet explores the upstairs rooms of her holiday house. Delighted to discover a name painted on a child's cot, she imagines a previous occupant sleeping in the room and then she meditates on the current troubles in Ireland. The distance between *the child who slept peacefully* (34) and the *murdered* (30) is starkly visible in the objects which hold their bodies, the cot and the coffins. You might like to trace the words which are associated with the cot and see how they build up the sense of a cherished and protected childhood. Peter's future seemed full of promise, like the girl taking a new dress from the box, like the poet herself exploring the holiday house. If it was otherwise, if he became one of the *deaths in alleyways and on doorsteps* (31) the poet prefers not to know.

Names carved on tombstones are *Inscriptions* and the poem's title refers to the names both on the cot and on coffins. The *importance* (26) of naming is challenged by *how important it is/not to name* (28–29). The loving care which preserved the cot inscription conflicts with the *name-eating elements* (45) which attack the tomb inscriptions. Contradictions and abrupt mood swings force us to face the poet's unanswered question *what comfort can there be* (39).

Throughout the poems in *Writing in a Time of Violence* one is conscious of warfare just out of sight and violence waiting to strike. The poems are not overtly political but private lives are shadowed by what is happening in public. The poems resonate with political meaning.

22–24 The perception in these lines moves to the child's viewpoint as he falls asleep, his eyes on the ray of dazzling moonlight across the ocean.

47 The poem ends with a question mark. Compare this hesitancy with the assertive tone of the final line of *That the Science of Cartography is Limited* (p.118).

Anna Liffey

I want a poem I can grow old in. I want a poem I can die in. In writings and interviews during the early 1990s Boland repeats this desire many times. She was still living *in my late forties* (83) in the house in the suburbs of Dublin to which she had moved in the second year of her marriage but feeling that

> The fragments and contradictions which had tormented my youth as a poet – issues of Irishness and of womanhood and the more subtle issues of an ethical identity – were beginning to find some repose. (*Object Lessons*, pp.229–230)

With difficulty, with a sense *of a theme just out of sight*, she tried to find ways of writing about *the ageing body*. She wanted to record *the accurate detail of time passing . . . My daughters' shadows in the garden, for instance, now grown longer than my own* (*Object Lessons*, p.209).

The narrative line of the poem follows the River Liffey from its source where it *rises in rush and ling heather* (13) to the city of Dublin and *under thirteen bridges to the sea* (32). Rain *moving east from the hills* (19) accompanies the river as it flows down into the Irish Sea (130-138) and then returns to the Dublin hills to start the process all over again.

> Follow the rain
> Out to the Dublin hills.
> Let it become the river. (164–166)

In the Liffey she found an image which expressed her sense of belonging to a country and its history and at the same time an image for herself as a poet and woman. The river is both *source* and *mouth* (81). Its continual flowing out to sea and replenishment at source suggest an allegory of presence and loss. Its winding course makes a *sign* (73,89) on the land which reflects her achievements as a mother and a writer. *I make this mark* (90). Its dissolution mirrors her consciousness of ceasing to be a presence in the physical world.

The Liffey is a narrator *Re-telling of a city* (28). It *finds/names* (66), *made* (131) *names* (131), *bestowed* (132) *names* (131). Like the Liffey, Boland is a poet, a *Maker* (36) although it has taken her *a suffered life* (93) to become *the mouth of it* (94). Starting with

... no children. No country.
I did not know the name for my own life   (48–9)

she bore daughters. She created *One name. Then the other one* (54). She made an image of herself, *A woman in a doorway* (60), and placed the image inside her own creation *a figure in a poem* (63). What does the river share with her life and where do the differences lie? You might like to start by tracing the words relating to creation and articulation and consider how they link the poet and the river. *Name* is the most repeated word, but note also *source, sign, mark* and *mouth*. Or you could compare the destiny of water with her sense of growing older.

The link between the Liffey and the poet is reinforced by repetition; repetition of single words (*home, patience, lost*) and key phrases like *A woman in a doorway*. More subtly Boland uses syntactically parallel phrases:

A woman in the doorway of a house.
A river in the city of her birth.   (9–10)

or

I take this sign
And I make this mark.   (89–90)

Even the seabirds flying in from the coast become another link in the poet's *arguments* (98) that language

needs to say –
What the body means –   (87–88)

that *The body is a source. Nothing more* (172); that

The body of an ageing woman
Is a memory.   (106–107)

Language and memory, the two ideas move and merge throughout the poem. If the poet has difficulty expressing the ageing body,

... to find a language for it
Is as hard
As weeping ...   (108–110)

the River Liffey which is a *Maker of ... remembrances* (36–37) has difficulty holding onto memory. *Which water – ... Remembers the other?*

(102–104). Uncertainties and insecurities underly the poem. They run beneath the placid narration which describes the Liffey's passage through history and landscape. Language *fails* (86); is *no shelter* (116); *cannot do it for us* (179).The word *if* reoccurs several times. Sentences end with question marks, culminating in the final question *Where is home now?* (163). What is the effect of these moments of doubt, difficulty and loss?

It is not only physical decay and dissolution which she has to face. Like all rivers *going home* (178) to *Their own nothingness* (177) it is the destiny of the Liffey to be swallowed by the Irish Sea which will give back *Only wordlessness* (133). Boland praises the Liffey's *patience* (33,78) and *powerlessness* (79) as she recognizes that her body also *seeks its own dissolution* (174). She has to accept, after *a suffered life* (93), after what has taken her *All my strength to do* (62) that she no longer owns her own creations. Her children are *Growing up* (156) and the words which *she once loved* (118) belong to others.

How does she face this destiny? Will she become *A lost soul* (168) like the waters which lose themselves in rivers, seas and rain? The word *lost* is repeated at line 187, yet the tone of the final stanza remains reflective and gentle. The *phrases/Of the ocean ... console* (181–183) countering the visible decay in a woman's body with the belief that *love will not diminish us* (180). What do you think is lost? What remains? *In the end* she claims *it will not matter* (169–170). Her body was a *source*. (For what?) She was a *voice* (188). The word is powerfully positioned at the end of the poem and the final line sounds affirmative. Does the poem end in a mood of resignation or hopefulness?

The form and rhythms of the poem are wonderfully fluid. Like the river itself, lines wind and flow down the page, alternating longer narrative sections with liturgical chanting rhythms of praise (25–46) and with sinuously indented lines (65–94) whose shape reflects the *sign* of the river. As the poet faces the decisive moment between her past and her future a firmer mood emerges. Notice how the stanzas become regular and compact, the lines briefer and the rhythm more tightly held in the penultimate section. In the final stanza the rhythms relax again into fluid lines whose length and syntax shadow and express their meaning, her acceptance of her destiny.

Although she twice summons the river in the imperative mood, *Narrate such fragments for me* (38) and *Tell me* (124), her ceremonial, respectful mode of address *Maker of/Places, remembrances* (36–37) and

> Anna Liffey,
> Spirit of water,
> Spirit of place,   (125–127)

make her commands seem more like humble requests. The poem balances passages of description, narration and reflection. Is there a point when the mood becomes more decisive, a moment when the poet recognizes her future? Or do you feel that her destiny and that of the river are seamlessly interwoven throughout?

1 **Life** Anna Livia is the name of the deity of the River Liffey. 'Anna' means river and 'Livia' comes from Liphe or Life which does not apply to the river itself but to the plain westwards of Dublin through which the river runs as it makes its way from the mountains in County Wicklow to the sea.

69–71 Among the major events in Dublin's history were the arrival of Viking settlers in 837, the forcible imposition of English rule (*Redcoats* [70]) which lasted from the Sixteenth to the Twentieth century and the battles for Home Rule which achieved independence for the Republic of Ireland in the Twentieth century. Boland's father was the first Irish Ambassador to London.

71 **Four Courts** the fine eighteenth century building in which Dublin's law courts sit. It was burnt on 27 June 1922 on the outbreak of civil war.

80 **Callary to Islandbridge** Callary Bog lies in the Wicklow Mountains, near the source of the Liffey, while Islandbridge is on the outskirts of Dublin (see also line 31). The phrase describes the passage of the river from its sources to the city.

Approaches

Introduction

The feminist critic Juliet Mitchell has said of modern women writers:

> I do not think that we can live as human subjects without in some sense taking on a history. (*Women: The Longest Revolution: Essays on Feminism, Literature and Psychoanalysis*, p.294)

You will need to think carefully about this word 'history' for history is not merely a record of external events but describes the changes in our inner lives, our spiritual history, or what the nineteenth century poet Keats described as our *soul-making*. There may be a sense in which women poets are not so much inventing a new voice, as recovering an old one. If we look at early pre-Christian civilizations, women were thought to have unique powers of religious insight, in many ways even superior to men's. The ancient priestesses and oracles spoke with powerful authority. It seemed as if with the coming of the Christian religion, woman, like Echo in the Greek myth, suddenly lost her voice, except of course to imitate others – usually the voices of men. She was turned into either a saint or a sinner. She could 'serve' or 'suffer', but not speak. And so woman as an 'oracular' power was suppressed. A male-dominated priesthood condemned women who spoke of God as instruments of darkness and hurried many of them to the stake as witches or blasphemers. It has taken almost two thousand years for women to recover a spiritual voice and to reinsert their own identities into a male-directed ideology – to redirect the words of Plath in *The Colossus* (p.41):

> ... I have laboured
> To dredge the silt from your throat.   (8–9)

You will find that the voices which sound through this collection of six very different and yet similar women over several generations and across a changing spiritual landscape, reveal a mixture of confidence and anxiety. In the section, Individual Voices (p.231), these will be examined in a more formal and technical sense. History has taught women that poetry has been produced through an authoritative male

216

voice. Not until the last century when Romanticism rejected poetry as a kind of 'public utterance' and placed a new emphasis on private and subjective vision, were women able to break their silence. They have chosen to speak with voices 'other' than the male, and the suppressed wisdom of centuries has imbued their response with a rich and sensitive spirituality.

The Spiritual Perspective

The Religious Landscape

Here Emily Brontë and Emily Dickinson were breaking new ground. Solitary by nature, almost unknown and unpublished during their lifetimes, theirs was a rôle of unease; and for Brontë of subterfuge – pretending to be male – and of mental dislocation (see the section, The Rhetoric of Anguish, p.223). But they were not silenced; their poems survived. In matters of religion they had one advantage over later women poets in that the Christian faith was not yet seriously challenged. Writing before Darwin and the theory of evolution, Brontë's faith, though fiercely questioned, was never doubted. For Dickinson, brought up in a strictly Puritan family, God was still a primary preoccupation and need.

The four later poets are seen against a very different religious landscape. Two violent world wars collapsed the class system, brought women into the male workplace and finally into the priesthood. Ironically, the Christian faith was already in distress, assailed by science and a materialistic society. No poet was more sorely tested by modern doubt than Elizabeth Jennings, yet alone of the four twentieth century poets she has remained truest to orthodox faith. For Eavan Boland, Sylvia Plath and Carol Ann Duffy the moral values of Christianity have been absorbed into a wider structure of myth and history. In this section, we shall try to describe and assess the contribution each poet in the anthology makes to our further understanding of the spiritual perspective.

Passionate Faith vs Seeds of Doubt

First let us look at Brontë's mystical view, perhaps her most original contribution to women's poetry. Its origins are rooted in her melancholy nature and initially seen in *'And first an hour of mournful musing'* (p.4). This seems a cyclical poem in which Brontë is locked into a pattern of unmanageable moods. Only in later poems like *The Philosopher* (p.12) – a metaphysical debate on light and darkness in which Creation struggles to reach a truth *White as the sun, far, far more fair* (39) – and *The Prisoner* (p.19), a genuine 'out of the body' experience – do her mature visionary powers emerge. Nowadays we might describe such experiences as a kind of mania. How far do you think Brontë was a disturbed soul or just a deeply religious woman? There is undoubtedly a dark side to her faith. In poems like *'There let thy bleeding branch atone'* (p.10) and *'I see around me tombstones grey'* (p.11) we ask what does she need to atone for? She seems so racked by secret guilt and a distaste for her own body. (See the section, The Rhetoric of Anguish, p.223.) Yet whatever her reasons for such ungovernable feelings you will find it difficult not to see religion as the essence of her being. It is a passionate faith rarely seen again in women's poetry.

Activity

Begin by reviewing Dickinson's *'Safe in their Alabaster Chambers'* (p.24) and *'There's a certain Slant of light'* (p.25). Look at her suspicions about God's benevolence – even his existence – and then compare it with Brontë's firm expression of faith. Then make a careful comparison of Brontë's *Death* (p.15) with Dickinson's *'Because I could not stop for Death'* (p.30) where their unique differences of belief (and style) are so apparent.

Discussion

Through her Gondal stories (see p.1), Brontë could translate her passions into her heroes' extreme or unorthodox codes of behaviour but Dickinson was closely indoctrinated in the puritan ethics of humanity and restraint. Like Brontë, torn by adolescent conflict, she relates to a cruel God not with defiant gestures of faith but a sharp, sceptical humour. Her reductive irony is much more subversive of Christian faith. After numerous attempts to get her poetry published (she met with little success) Dickinson gradually withdrew into almost complete seclusion; she stopped going to church and wrote for herself alone. Brontë sees Nature as a barrier to the spiritual world, something restraining her from a blissful reunion with God, but for Dickinson the earth is Paradise enough were it not for God's *marauding Hand* (*'Immortal is an ample word'*, p.31 [7]) and she mocks certain hopes of resurrection. They have very different attitudes to suffering. Dickinson is prepared to *fit our Vision to the Dark* (*'We grow accustomed to the Dark'*, p.28 [7]) but Brontë is always uncompromising. Look at the way Dickinson relates time and eternity in *'Safe in their Alabaster Chambers'* (p.24).

Grand go the Years – in the Crescent – above them—
Worlds scoop their Arcs—
And Firmaments – row—
Diadems – drop – and Doges – surrender—
Soundless as dots – on a Disc of Snow—   (6–10)

Images of time, space, even snow, recall Brontë but here there is a sense of defeat. This difference is seen sharply in a comparison of *Death* (p.15) and *'Because I could not stop for Death'* (p.30). Both are great religious poems but while Brontë's is personal, full of passion and pain, Dickinson's, though none the less uniquely her own, has achieved an acceptance, distilling a lifetime's experience into a time-scheme of a single afternoon and into the fewest perfectly placed words. Note both poems end on the word *Eternity* but in such different moods, one in triumph, the other in dignified resignation.

Jennings: a Questioning Conscience

Between the poetry of Dickinson and Jennings almost a century has passed in which our religious consciousness has been profoundly disturbed. Jennings' adolescence was spent against the rise and fall of Nazism. Raised as a strict Roman Catholic, her faith prompted social obligations, yet she is first of all a poet. Opting out of traditional feminine rôles is still a source of anxiety resulting, as it did for Plath, in periods of mental anguish. Jennings' visit to Rome in 1955 was a moment of spiritual renewal. She has since compared writing poems to saying prayers. For her the sacramental duties of the Mass and the Eucharist are ways of formalizing her deepest experiences. Yet true faith is always questioned *even great faith leaves room for abysses* (*World I Have Not Made*, (p.71) [25]). In an introduction Jennings wrote to an anthology of British writers, she recalls asking herself:

... 'What is the Holy Ghost?' ... I had never heard of Hopkins
but I did imagine the Holy Spirit as an enormous bird
... I moved on to almost every other kind of query about my creed.
(*The Bloodaxe Book of Contemporary Women Poets*, p.99)

Her problem is 'How does abstract thought relate to common experience?' As an intellectual she was drawn to philosophers like Aquinas and Descartes. The big questions were bruising to the mind but clamoured to be answered.

Activity

Begin with Jennings' poem *The Climbers* (p.62) and then look at *Remembering Fireworks* (p.74). You will find that both poems are seeking to express difficult ideas in clear images. For insight into her conflicting views of Christianity compare *The World We Made* (p.79) with *World I Have Not Made* (p.71). Finally look at the poem *Thinking of Descartes* (p.77) and try to understand what she means by *those pure peaks* (13).

Discussion

Jennings rarely has flashes of insight. She depicts life as a tortuous climb whose motive for beginning has *grown obscure* (*The Climbers*, p.62 [14]). Often close to despair, we go on. Having resolved what she means by the peaks of experience, what might the abyss represent? Is our motive for climbing only our dread of falling into the abyss? Could love for each other only be another form of selfishness? The answer to these questions lies in her Catholicism. Only in Jennings' poetry in this collection will you see the truly Catholic conscience. She is never free from a sense of accountability for every lapse, constant self-scrutiny and a renunciation of possessions (she still lives a very frugal life). Yet in her poems we meet great human qualities – patience, tenderness, forgiveness, love. Her purity of expression touches us because it is *not a turning loose of emotion but an escape from emotion* (T.S. Eliot, 'Essay on Tradition and the Individual Talent', 1919) as is the ritual of prayer. She expresses complex things – lost childhood vision (*Remembering Fireworks*, p.74), the indifference of the gods (*Greek Statues*, p.72) in bare, clean language.

From Myth into History

The other three poets in the collection are supremely concerned with our 'mortality'. With Plath it is a *long wait for the angel* (*Black Rook in Rainy Weather*, p.38 [39]) which when it appears comes in the guise of death itself; with Boland we inhabit *a landscape in which you know you are mortal* (*Outside History*, p.113 [10]) and with Duffy we find that *no explanations tremble on our flesh* (*The Dolphins*, p.89 [8]).

Activity

With this theme of mortality in mind, review your reading of the following poems: Plath's *Black Rook in Rainy Weather* (p.37), Boland's *The Dolls' Museum in Dublin* (p.118) and *The Making of an Irish Goddess* (p.111) and lastly Duffy's *Ash Wednesday 1984* (p.90) and *The Dolphins* (p.89).

Discussion

Speaking with a singular and disturbing voice and with a power some-times of a being possessed by some external force, Plath is drawn to the passion of the priestly rôle but not its faith. Like Jennings she was influenced by the Jesuit poet Gerard Manley Hopkins and in particular *The Windhover*, a poem about Christ. In *Black Rook in Rainy Weather* (p.37) she employs Christian imagery – the bird is a miracle, a Pentecostal fire, and the bird/Christ image which we saw in Brontë's *Stars* (p.17) appears also in her *A Winter Ship* (p.39) – *an albatross of frost* (26). (See Notes to line 26, p.158.) But the Christian faith is no more sacred to her than the myths of Greece (*The Colossus*, p.41) or Rome (*The Arrival of the Bee Box*, p.48) – all myths are equal in her search for expression.

Boland's sources too are deep in the past, in Irish and classical legend in which she finds no contradiction so that Ceres and Persephone walk together with Anna Liffey. However, for her, spiritu-ality is part of the living present. The homely tasks of wrapping a parcel, making lace or carrying a bucket create a pattern across the generations and thus assume a mythical significance. Though living for much of her life in Catholic Ireland, she sees Easter in *The Dolls' Museum in Dublin* (p.118) as only the background to a deeper interest – the suffering of women and men. Irish religious conflict resounds throughout her poetry but she does not need the re-enforcing authority of Christianity. She does not prescribe but merely records the voice of the dispossessed.

221

Though she questions its dogma and beliefs, the Roman Catholic faith braces Duffy's imagination. The language and sacraments of religion are in her blood although she recognizes that the male Catholic view has not been kind to women, nor does it convey easy death. The ritual of prayer, however, remains vital to her artistic expression. Duffy is intolerant of bigotry and superstition, as seen in her poem *Ash Wednesday 1984* (p.90):

> ... Miracles and shamrocks
> and transubstantiation are all my ass.
> For Christ's sake, do not send your kids to Mass.   (18–20)

but this is an attack, not on Christian faith, but on its vulgar trappings which can be a cheap substitute. *Making Money* (p.96), *A Healthy Meal* (p.87), and *Psychopath* (p.92) are like demonstrations of deadly sins, the results of greed, gluttony and lust, when Christian morality is abandoned. She brings a fresh vision to the Christian story in *The Virgin Punishing the Infant* (p.94). In *Prayer* (p.101) she expresses the basic human need for all of us to speak to our Creator. She also has a mystical side to her; her wonder at light as a language which speaks to our souls. (*The Grammar of Light*, p.100 reminds us of Brontë's *Stars*, p.17 and Jennings' *The Diamond Cutter*, p.72.) *The Dolphins* (p.89) is a great religious poem because it expresses a complexity of the spirit through an universal image (as Dickinson does in *'Because I could not stop for Death*, p.30). There is no explanation only a simple recognition of man's sinfulness; only a pitiful image of his lost soul and fall from grace – *We were blessed and now we are not blessed* (*The Dolphins*, p.89 [9]).

If Jennings and Boland have achieved a hard-won serenity, Duffy has acquired a humorous balance, a kind of metaphysical wit. All of these poets have attained a spiritual harmony: they have moved away from the merely personal and subjective towards a broader socio-historical perspective. They have progressed from Plath, whose manic genius is undenied but whose wounds now seem almost like a lapse of literary taste. They are totally unlike Brontë and Dickinson deploring their loneliness, cut off from men and in cultural exile, but they share a common spirituality which is specifically rooted in their being women who have emerged from myth into history.

The Rhetoric of Anguish

God Almighty said: 'I will produce a self-working automatic machine for enduring suffering, which shall be capable of the largest amount of suffering in a given space', and he made woman. But he wasn't satisfied that he [had] reached the highest perfection so he ... made a woman of genius – and he was satisfied. (*The Letters of Olive Schreiner* 1876–1920)

All six poets might well understand Schreiner's extreme statement, for many of the poems in the collection are about private suffering. Perhaps this raises the question 'Why do women need to communicate their anguish so pointedly?'

In examining the history of women's literature, we are confronted by the sense of so many unrecorded lives. Is it that since the last century women have at last been able to release long-repressed anger? Could it just be that women feel mental and emotional pain more than men? In searching for explanations we must confront the fact that for women of previous generations society somehow introduced the idea which called them to suppress their personal ambitions in the name of service to others. For the vast majority of women 'being yourself' was synonymous with 'being selfish'. What then of the woman poet who above all is called to fulfil her own special identity and for whom poetry is the essence of her being? One answer may be that in the past she has carried an enormous burden of guilt and her development as a writer has depended on how she was able to resolve this conflict. Much of the anguish seen here may be an off-loading of centuries of guilt feelings.

Brontë and Dickinson had been told that women, if they resisted total marginalization, could only write about their private and domestic lives. Theirs could only be a small 'personal' voice – all too painfully true for they had been denied any cultural history of their own. Hence they were driven into explorations of childhood or Gothic fantasy – the equivalent of fairy tales for adults. Although they did not marry and thus avoided the responsibilities of child-bearing, the severe restraints of socially sanctioned behaviour in a male-dominated orthodoxy was for them deadly in its consequences resulting in complete withdrawal and severe dislocation of the personality. It is also disturbing to note that Plath and Jennings also experienced periods of mental anguish. The lesson of history seems to suggest that such was the outcome of social conditioning. Yet a case may be made for the idea that poets are by nature over-sensitive to emotional stress, closer to the elemental moments of life. Brontë certainly showed signs of acute depression from her late teens. There are signs of sexual fear, despair even self-loathing in her work. Dickinson also withdrew into an inner world, squirrelling away her poems and refusing to leave her home. For both poets, writing provided not a means of communicating anguish, but a protected opportunity for its concealment.

Jennings achieved early academic success but between the 1950s and 1960s her work was dropped by critics, partly because she refused to remain silent about her mental upheavals. Courageously she fought her way back to a fresh, desentimentalized lyricism. The story of Plath's life is well-known. She pushed herself to succeed in many areas, not just writing, but she now seems the archetype of Schreiner's woman of genius, specially programmed for suffering. If this anthology ended with *Edge* (p.59) it would be a bleak picture indeed, but in fact it emerges into the light with three living poets who have come relatively safely through the birth-pains of women's writing – Jennings with a religious serenity, Duffy with a witty, wry detachment from personal pain, and Boland with a rich humanity. It would seem that at last, women poets are able to live with their own consciences.

Living without God

Activity

From the previous section, The Spiritual Perspective, (pp.217–222) you will have discovered poems which describe the misery of not understanding God's purpose. Now, look at some examples of the poets who find a loss of paternalistic authority difficult and then decide which have come to terms with this. You can begin with Dickinson's *'Over the Fence'* (p.24), *'There's a certain Slant of light'* (p.25) and *'Presentiment – is that long Shadow – on the Lawn'* (p.31); Jennings' *World I Have Not Made* (p.71); Plath's *The Arrival of the Bee Box* (p.48) and Duffy's *Small Female Skull* (p.99).

Discussion

Religious doubt in the Nineteenth century led to an artistic crisis in which poets turned inwards to personal grief and private wounds.

Dickinson grows alarmed by *that long Shadow* (*'Presentiment – is that long Shadow – on the Lawn'* [1]) and a scolding God (see *'Over the Fence'*). In *World I Have Not Made*, Jennings grieves about an apparently heartless Creator:

> ... It is hard, hard,
> even with free faith outlooking boundaries,
> to come to terms with obvious suffering.   (13–15)

In *Words of Absolution* (p.91), Duffy too looks with anxiety at old age and death and all the unanswered questions *After/ your night prayers what should you do?* (28-29) *What do you mean/by the resurrection of the body?* (12–13). Brontë unable to rationalize her mood-changes by knowledge of modern psychology, wrestles with metaphysics and theology *warring night and day* (*The Philosopher*, p.13 [18]). With Plath (see *The Arrival of the Bee Box*) the questions seem like bees inside her head, driving her mad:

> I have simply ordered a box of maniacs ...
> ... I will set them free.
> The box is only temporary.   (23–36)

Jennings wakes in the night with questions about existence and identity (see *In the Night*, p.67) feeling that from adolescence she has been unable *To dream but must learn to know* (*The World We Made*, p.80 [52]). In Duffy's *Small Female Skull* the woman watches herself weep in a mirror – *they will think I have lost my mind* (18) – but it is significant that she ends the anguish not by thoughts of suicide, but by laughing at her own self-indulgence. Dickinson and Plath seem the most unreconciled to living without some kind of paternal authority and are perhaps the most troubled spirits.

Living with the Female Body

Nineteenth century women were inhibited in writing about sex and the human body. It is not until the Twentieth century that we find poets trying to write openly about women's physical experiences. Boland shares with Plath the urge to find a language which will express the female body. It is central to Plath's poetry. The extremity of her emotional swings from creative to destructive is imaged in how and with whom she shares her body. Notice how freely she uses it in poems of love and how vulnerable she feels to attack and invasion by men cutting, smashing and dismembering it in her hostile poems. Boland is more accepting of the physical demands of sexuality, child-bearing and ageing but she recognizes a fellow creative spirit. After Plath's suicide she wrote:

> From now on I would write, at least partly, in the shadow of that act: unsettled and loyal. Other poets – men – moved easily among the models of the poet's life, picking and choosing. I chose this one – not to emulate but to honour. Not simply for the beautiful, striving language of the poems when I came to read them. But because I could see increasingly the stresses and fractures between a poet's life and a woman's. (*Object Lessons*, p.113)

Activity

Try to find one poem from each poet where women pause to examine their attitudes towards their bodies. Some poems you might explore include *'There let thy bleeding branch atone'* (p.10), *Metaphors* (p.41), *The Woman Changes her Skin* (p.104), *Tulips* (p.45) and *Recognition* (p.88).

Discussion

A distinctive feature in the poems is the frequency with which women express distaste at their own bodies. In *'There let thy bleeding branch atone'*, Brontë presents a disturbing image of self-mutilation. The image of the severed branch reminds us of that violent image in *Wuthering Heights* where Lockwood cuts the child's wrist on the broken window-pane. One aspect of clinical depression is cutting or slashing the body, almost a primitive ritual of atonement. Brontë speaks of *wounds that will not heal again* (*'I see around me tombstones grey'*, p.11 [10]) and in *The Prisoner* (p.19) she speaks of the body as a cage of the soul. Plath surveys dismembered bodies in *Two Views of a Cadaver Room* (p.40), a theme which recurs in *Lady Lazarus* (p.54) and *Tulips*. Even Plath's attitude to pregnancy seems ambiguous. The woman's body in *Metaphors* is comic, even surrealistic – *A melon strolling on two tendrils* (3). The cosy image of motherhood seen in *Morning Song* (p.45) – *cow-heavy and floral/In my Victorian nightgown* (13–14) seems alien. In *Lady Lazarus* (p.56) she strips the body down to what remains after incineration –

A cake of soap,
A wedding ring,
A gold filling.   (76–78)

How extreme do you find these images?

Transformation is at the heart of Boland's poem, *The Woman Changes her Skin*. The woman applies make-up to change her external appearance as a snake sheds its skin to reveal a new skin lying beneath. Is sexuality being imposed on a woman and if so, by whom? Male expectations? Group or advertising pressures? Or is the woman's inner sexuality being liberated? In *Suburban Woman: a Detail* (p.107) something is *softening the definitions* (37) of the woman's body; it is losing its *detail* (26). The poem's narrator seems uncertain about the meaning of these softly blurring changes but the voice of the tree, *Look at me* (28), links her with all women who have lived previously, *full-skirted, human* (30). Her *flesh* (40) registers their past experience, a premonition of her own mortality. As you read Boland's poems you will find further instances of her respect for women's ageing bodies and the meanings they hold: the *cold rosiness* (10) of the hands of the Achill Woman; *the marks of childbirth* (*The Making of an Irish Goddess*, p.111 [16]) the *wounds* (1) and *cracks* (2) on the dolls in *The Dolls' Museum in Dublin* (p.118).

In *Tulips*, Plath's attitude lies somewhere between denial and celebration of the body. Peaceful in hospital at the beginning of the poem, she has *given* (6) her *body to surgeons* (7) and nurses *tend it* (15). She wants to be *utterly empty* (30), to *efface myself* (48). The tranquil tone of her resignation lies partly in the association of body images with water, always a calming presence in Plath's poetry. Her body is cared for gently *as water tends to the pebbles* (16). She is a *thirty-year-old cargo boat* (22) who has let things slip and is about to *sink out of sight* (27) except that the demands of her husband and child catch on her skin like fish *hooks* (21). As she reduces her shape to *a cut-out paper shadow* (46), the slightest possible physical presence, the intrusive tulips alert her to the *red blooms* (61) of her own heart which *opens and closes* (60). Do you feel she arrives at an equilibrium, accepting the role of wife and mother? Or does the poem end in evasion, a denial of health as *a country far away* (63)?

Duffy, like Plath, contemplates bare, unaccommodated woman in *Standing Female Nude* (p.86) but gives to her a dignity and precious self-hood. In *Making Money* (p.96) she even allows the prostitute Kim, *nun, nurse, nanny/nymph on a credit card* (15–16) a measure of dignity, for in acquiring a different persona, is she not a kind of poet?

A partial answer to the question 'Why do women hate their bodies?', may be found in the mirror references in the poems, this one from *Mirrors* (p.66) by Jennings:

... halls of mirrors where
In every place we look we see our stare
Taunting our own identities ...   (9–11)

In Duffy's *Recognition*, the middle-aged woman is shocked by her neglected overweight image in the mirror and apologizes to herself. In *Small Female Skull* (p.99) the woman sees in the mirror something like a ventriloquist's doll. Mirrors induce ambivalent feelings, vanity with insecurity, admiration with fault-finding, truth with disguises, seeking one's true self but also conforming to some ideal and therefore unattainable stereotype.

Men appear as a major source of anguish in relation to how women see their bodies yet the poets seem contradictory in their attitudes to them. Women need men but they also resent domination and/or patronage. It seems that women have difficulty being themselves in men's presence; perhaps they feel they must adjust to some doll-like substitute. First they conform to their father's – or God's – wishes. Consider for instance the influence of Patrick Brontë on his daughters. The father image appears obsessively in Plath's poems. In *The Colossus* (p.41) she rejects his gigantic image and in *Daddy* (p.51) she tries to root out his influence. Hatred and love seem inextricably combined, *Every woman adores a Fascist* (48). Plath only survives by transferring her allegiance to her husband. At the same time she loathes her slavish dependence. In *The Applicant* (p.49) she presents herself as *a living doll* (33) applying for the post of wife, *Will you marry it?* (14,22,40). Why should such a woman of genius feel such devastating lack of self-esteem?

This is perhaps one of the unanswered questions in the collection. Even Boland and Duffy do not provide us with satisfactory answers. But in reading poems like *The Dolls' Museum in Dublin* (p.118) we begin to feel women distancing themselves from their dependence on men and their obsession with their physical appearance. Boland refers to

Booted officers and *Their mistresses* (10) and shows us centuries of suffering:

> The wounds are terrible. The paint is old.
> The cracks along the lips and on the cheeks
> cannot be fixed ... (1–3)

The lines may of course equally refer to women's obsessive dread of growing old – yet she hints at an approaching end of this torment *It is twilight in the dolls' museum* (33). Duffy too explores the idea of women as dolls in *Psychopath* (p.92). The girl on the roundabout with her *candyfloss* (12) complexion is a stereotype of the pop culture of the 1950s. Her murderer sees her as a woman with marketable potential: *A girl like that should have a paid-up solitaire* (55). *The Ladies' Man* (50) know(s) *what women want* (19). Though her end is brutal the girl has a kind of revenge on her killer. The poem ends with a picture of a scrambled personality *Awopbopalooboopalopbimbam* (64) and we are left with a sense of loathing and pity.

Living with Others

Unmarried, childless, living out their lives in their fathers' houses, it is not surprising that the relationships depicted in the poems of the nine-teenth century poets should be either intimate or imagined. Brontë never seems to have had a close relationship with anyone outside her own family and her love poems are about imaginary figures, many from the Gondal saga. What her poetry shares with Dickinson is a sense of passionate, unrequited love. While continuing to write about their families, twentieth century poets explore a wider set of relationships. Duffy and Jennings create a gallery of characters: climbers, old ladies, diamond cutters, interrogators, teachers, models, gourmets, menopausal women, psychopaths and foreigners whom they present sometimes warmly, sometimes critically and sometimes with detatched ambiguity. Boland too has a series of portraits. Many are shadowy, anonymous figures from history whom she brings to our attention sympathetically by describing the way they moved or a gesture they made. Plath tends to concentrate on intimate relationships but in *The Applicant* (p.49) she creates a narrator who, like Duffy's Head of English, condemn themselves with every word they utter.

Activity

What are the poets' attitudes towards the characters they create in *Psychopath* (p.92) by Duffy and *My Grandmother* (p.70) by Jennings?

Discussion

The possessive *My* in Jennings' title suggests a close and warm involvement so it comes as a surprise to find she recalls her relationship with her grandmother as distant, *there was no need of love* (6). Her grandmother *kept* (1) herself apart, like an antique. When she ceased to polish her objects and they could no longer give back her reflection, *There was nothing* (17), as though the grandmother related only to her antiques, *her best things* (14). Does this coldness justify the child's instinctive refusal to go out with her or do you feel that the poet is right to feel guilty? There is tension in the poem between *used* and *need*. The child is afraid of being used like the antique objects but realizes when she is older that her grandmother *never used* (22) them. She *needed* (23) them. The repetition of *needed* and *used* links back to *there was no need of love* (6). Notice how it is qualified by the phrase *as if to prove* (5). What does the adult recognize which the child (and grandmother?) failed to understand?

Because *Psychopath* is written in the first person it generates a degree of empathy with the speaker. We see things from his point of view. The story unfolds in flashbacks and we have to piece together from the psychopath's casual comments exactly what has happened. Do you find the point of view shifting at any point in the poem? The girl who will end up in the water (note the repetition of *She is in the canal* [4,46]) and the fish which is spilled out of water to die on the grass seem linked at the critical moment by her silent stare (38). Sympathy moves to the victim. Yet the murder is immediately followed by a description of the psychopath's destructive childhood and early sexual experiences. Does this create understanding for his terrible deeds? Or is Duffy subtly, clinically, allowing him to reveal himself in all his egocentric amorality? The voice of the psychopath is cocky and arrogant: *A town like this would kill me* (33), *I touch it/and love myself* (14-15), *Deep down I'm talented* (58) but emotionally detached, *Bang in the centre of my skull,/there's a strange coolness* (61-62). Is his boast, *I'm no nutter* (59) confirmation or ironic condemnation of a character whom Duffy labels *Psychopath*?

All the poets in the selection write about love. What it means to them sometimes becomes most apparent in moments of absence and loss.

Activity

Compare the reactions to bereavement and loss in Brontë's *'And first an hour of mournful musing'* (p.4), Jennings' *It Is Not True?* (p.81) and Dickinson's *'My life closed twice before its close'* (p.32).

Discussion

What is noticeable in Brontë is the absence of sustained grief. She rejoices because love is changed into a *glorious star* (8). For Dickinson, being denied love was a calamity which left her numbed and despairing. She was constrained to hide her feelings in poems which articulate the powerlessness of women whose love is denied expression. Feminist criticism sees in her disjointed grammar and broken phrases signs of the pressures on women in the Nineteenth century to be silent about sexual passion. Poems apparently as light-weight as *'South Winds jostle them'* (p.23) have been read as covertly expressing sexual desire.

When Jennings lost her mother, death became real to her for the first time. *Death is not true* (25) until *someone close . . . dies* (13–14) . This is similar to Dickinson's *Parting is all we know* (7). Death may remain unknowable (*Countries untried* [31] to Jennings, *hopeless to conceive* [5] to Dickinson) but both poets react to the shock of losing someone they love with a growing awareness of what Jennings calls *Our final goings* (22) and Dickinson, *Immortality* (3). It is a measure of their grief and their love. Compare the final lines of each poem. Do you find Brontë's confident faith a sign that she was less involved in human relationships?

Individual Voices: Language, Imagery, and Form

Six poets – six women – six voices, all very individual. Do the differences and similarities between them arise from the way women experienced their lives, whether in the Nineteenth or Twentieth centuries, or is it more to do with each poet's individual voice? What do we mean, after all, by the 'voice' of the poet?

Partly it is a matter of language reflecting the time at which the poems were written. You are unlikely to confuse late twentieth century *Megabucks* and *cellular telephone* (Duffy), *plastic-pillowed trolley* (Plath) or *can of Coke* (Boland) with Brontë's *worlds of solemn light* and *Time's all-severing wave*. Brontë and Plath are both impassioned voices but whereas Brontë writes in ornate, Victorian phrases (*deep glooms, hatred's tiger glare, rapturous pain*) Plath uses contemporary colloquialisms (*you bastard, it feels like hell, it's your last resort*).

Partly it is a matter of imagery. Brontë and Dickinson take their images from the domestic sphere and from Nature. To Dickinson the passage between life and death is a door between two rooms, a fly buzzing or an afternoon's outing. To both women Nature is a revelatory blessing, a benign glimpse of the spiritual world whether as stars or winds or bluebells in Brontë or a prairie or the flight of a robin in Dickinson. What is absent in their poetry is any mention of public events. *Jason – sham – too* ('Finding is the first Act', p.31 [8]) writes Dickinson, dismissively turning her back on worldly achievement as she does in 'The Show is not the Show' (p.32) and 'I'm Nobody! Who are you?' (p.25). Her humour mocks the public sphere from which she is excluded, calling it a *Show*. Brontë's poems do not even acknowledge its existence. Yet in many of their poems there is a yearning tone, a sense of restricted lives from which the only escape is into stoical silence, lonely endurance and a pleasure in Nature.

As women entered more fully into the public domain we might expect this to register in their writings. Do the twentieth century poems seem less excluded from public events, less restricted to private experience? It was important to Plath to widen her intensely private subject matter to include history and to relate her sense of personal persecution to the Holocaust. In a recording for radio she argued that *Experience shouldn't be a kind of shut box* and that a poet's private pain *should be relevant to Dachau and Hiroshima*. For this she has been both acclaimed and attacked. Like Plath, Boland also wishes to relate ordinary daily life to history, to the troubles of Ireland, past and present. Jennings places herself in the mainstream of European intellectual and cultural traditions by her wide-ranging references, from Oxford to Rome and from Descartes and Chardin to Van Gogh and Op art.

Activity

To what extent does the imagery of Dickinson's *'I heard a Fly buzz –
when I died'* (p.29) and Plath's *Lady Lazarus* (p.54) draw on ideas of
public and private worlds?

Discussion

The patients in both poems are seriously ill; close to death in
Dickinson, recovering from suicide in Plath. But the place where the
patients lie is quite different. Dying at home, surrounded by friends
waiting for *that last Onset* (7) was as normal in the Nineteenth century
as being nursed in hospital is in the Twentieth. Dickinson's images are
legal (her father and brother were both lawyers), drawn from Nature
(the moment of death is like the calm between *Heaves of Storm* [4])
and domestic. The borderland between life and death is imaged as
Windows (15). The unexpected guide into eternity is an uncertain and
stumbling *Fly* (12).

Plath's images group into three clusters: the concentration camps in
Nazi Germany (the phoenix rises from the ashes of the concentration-
camp furnaces); the biblical story of Lazarus and a strip-tease show.
The range of her imagery, drawn from mythology, Christianity, history
and theatrical entertainment, is striking compared to Dickinson's
narrow image base. If this is a result of the freedom of twentieth-
century women's lives compared to the restrictions of the Nineteenth
century, has Plath taken this freedom too far? Has she the right to use
the Holocaust for her imagery? The critic Harold Bloom called this
poem *a gratuitous and humanly offensive appropriation of the
imagery of Jewish martyrs in Nazi death camps* and he also quotes
Helen Vendler's *a tantrum of style . . . a centrifugal spin to further and
further reaches of outrage* in his introduction to a collection of essays
entitled *Sylvia Plath* (p.3).Other critics, however, regard it as one of
her great poems.

Plath's images may seem to have little connection either with the
poem's subject or with other images in the poem until you recognize
that they relate in psychological rather than realistic ways. The image
clusters reveal a state of mind, like the language of marketing and
salesmanship in *The Applicant* (p.49) or the references to the dominating size of the statue in *The Colossus* (p.41). In *Daddy* (p.51),
imagery from fairy tales, statues, Nazis and vampires expresses
Plath's sense of constriction and repression by dominating males.

Other poets, however, develop a single image throughout the whole poem, as Jennings does in *Fountain* (p.69) and *The Diamond Cutter* (p.72) and as Boland does in *Anna Liffey* (p.122).

Activity

What similarities and differences do you find in the choice of language and use of images in *The World We Made* (p.79) by Jennings and *The Pomegranate* (p.114) by Boland?

Discussion

The subject of both poems is the same, the loss of innocence, although it is approached from different viewpoints. Jennings looks back on her own childhood while Boland reflects on her daughter's emerging adulthood. Both poets address the reader in plain vocabulary and a confiding voice, allowing us, as it were, to overhear their thoughts. Each poem has one central image: the bottle of cochineal and the pomegranate. Jennings introduces the cochineal dye realistically into her narrative as she remembers how the children painted a totem pole bright red and named it after the colouring essence. In the children's imaginations the pole becomes a God, taking on a capital C. When their father attacks their belief 'cochineal' is reduced to a colouring essence and the first letter of the word becomes lower case again. In the structure of the poem cochineal develops from a concrete object to symbolize the imaginative world the children created and lost as they *Shrank into teenagers* (50). For her central image Boland takes a symbol from a classical legend. We need to know the story of Persephone if we are to understand how Boland uses the pomegranate to symbolize what is gained and what is lost as children enter their teenage years. Two poems, alike in subject, sharing an easy vocabulary and colloquial tone, are distinguished by their choice of imagery. Jennings creates a unique image within the confines of the poem while Boland chooses a traditional symbol.

Another way of identifying a poet's voice is to study her use of rhyme, rhythm and form. You will probably find it easier to spot the rhymes in the nineteenth century poems because both poets use full rhymes although Dickinson sometimes moves to subtler half-rhymes. Look, for instance, at the rhymes in '*Because I could not stop for Death*' (p.30). They fall on the second and fourth lines and move from full rhymes *me/ty* (2,4) to half-rhymes *Ring/Sun* (10,12) and *chill/Tulle* (14,16). In the penultimate verse the same word *Ground* (18,20) insistently repeats (to what effect?) and in the last verse rhyme all but disappears.

Since then – 'tis Centuries – and yet
Feels shorter than the Day
I first surmised the Horses' Heads
Were toward Eternity—   (21–24)

We are left with an unresolved rhyme. The grammar and syntax of the final lines seem to offer the reader a clear statement about the poet's situation but the lack of a firm closing rhyme undercuts her mood of serene acceptance by leaving the ending open, hinting at a lack of finality. Neither her journey nor her understanding of what is happening is complete.

In the Twentieth century, poets enjoy more freedom to experiment with poetic forms than in the Nineteenth century and the poems in this selection range from Duffy's choice of the traditional sonnet form in *Prayer* (p.101) to Jennings' use of free verse in *Still Life* (p.83). Yet Jennings can be rigorously formal. She shares with the early Plath a fascination in experimenting with widely contrasting poetic forms. Blank verse in *The Climbers* (p.62) and *World I Have Not Made* (p.71); symmetrically paired rhymes in *My Grandmother* (p.70); asymmetrically paired rhymes in *Mirrors* (p.66); quatrains in *The World We Made* (p.79); terza rima in *Kings* (p.63); couplets in *Choices* (p.68) and triplets in *It Is Not True?* (p.81); repetitive lines in *The Interrogator* (p.73) and intricate patterns in *Beyond Possession* (p.64). Whatever she writes is fashioned with scrupulous care and held in tight patterns. Nothing is loose; experience is refashioned and controlled by technique. Consider, for example, the rhymes in *Kings*. The first and third lines in each verse take their rhyme from the middle line of the preceding verse. And if that were not sufficiently intricate, Jennings varies the pattern of the final two lines, adding an additional 'ing' rhyme (*worshipping* [12]) which delays the closing rhyme (*friends* [13]) and brings the poem to a polished but disconcerting end.

Activity

Try reading aloud *'No coward soul is mine'* (p.20) by Brontë and *Outside History* (p.113) by Boland. What effect does the presence or absence of rhyme, rhythm and form have on the poems?

Discussion

Brontë's poem has regular, rhyming stanzas, end-stopped lines and a powerful rhythm with alternating lines of three and five heavily stressed iambic feet. The clarity, the forthrightness of rhyme, rhythm and stanzas help to establish the defiant tone of the poem. Consider the two final stanzas where she affirms her faith in *Heaven's glories* (3). The line *And thou wert left alone* (23) sounds cold and hard. It consists mainly of curt monosyllables and the stresses are emphasized because each falls on the heavy beat of an iambic foot. This harshness immediately contrasts with the following gentle line *Every Existence would exist in thee* (24). Reading this aloud, you will find the word *Every* refuses to fit a regular iambic foot. How would you scan the line *Since thou art Being and Breath* (27)? It does not conform exactly and the slightly off-beat sound helps to create a sense of the strangeness and otherness which is the essence of Brontë's God.

Although Boland's poem has regular three-line stanzas it seems freer. The lines follow no set pattern of metrical feet and are unrhymed. In an interview with Jan Garden Castro (printed in *Tampa Review*, 10, Spring 1995) Boland explained that her stanzas are *slightly deformalized*. The apparent freedom of her style comes from an apprenticeship in traditional poetic forms. Awareness and respect for traditional forms lie behind her writing. *I'm a conservative technician ... I'm interested in the use of metrical shadows, but I don't use metre – very, very rarely.* The opening line of *Outside History* (p.113) has five stresses, which echoes blank verse. The following lines have different lengths and a different number of stresses but they continue the same steady narrative tone which is a quality of blank verse. The ending of each line coincides with its meaning until we reach the fifth line and find its opening words *our pain did* (5) depend upon the word *before* in the previous line. Our understanding of the fourth line, which had appeared to be self-contained, is changed. It is the first intimation that the poem is considering the difference between being outside and inside the ordeal of history. The light which *happened/thousands of years before* (3-4) has become a measure of *our pain* (5).

When the positioning of words is no longer dictated by the requirements of rhythm and rhyme, effects are created by the way words and phrases are juxtaposed or cut off, repeated or contrasted, linked and reflected back on each other. The word *Outside* is given prominence in the title and becomes more important with each repetition. The slight variation in the repeated phrases in the closing line highlights the word *always* (21), conveying a sense of remorse. The word *always* appears also in the opening line. Does the verbal link suggest that the outside-inside division which the poem poses is perhaps less clear-cut? Are we sensing hesitation, the poet wondering whether she is an insider because she chooses *to be/part of that ordeal* (13–14) or remains an outsider because she is *always too late* (21)?

Activity

Compare Duffy's *The Dolphins* (p.89) with Plath's *Daddy* (p.51). What effect do the rhymes have?

Discussion

Daddy is thick with rhyme. The simple *oo* sound dominates the poem, following no regular pattern but hammering home the childish tone of the speaker. With *The Dolphins* it takes careful listening to hear the occasional half-rhymes (*began/man* [10,12]; *grooves/blows* [19,23]) yet these light touches are part of the grace of the dolphins. Duffy tends to use rhyme sparingly. *Ash Wednesday 1984* (p.90), for instance, seems unrhymed until the fourth stanza which has a tight rhyme scheme, stressing the difference between the poet's reflective musings and the voice of authority.

The shaping force in Duffy's poetry is her sense of form. If you look at any poem the visual patterns on the page appear more ordered than the looser lines of Plath or Boland and the shape has an effect on the content. You might like to think about what happens in the stanza breaks in *Head of English* (p.85). The insensitive personality of the speaker reveals itself in the way he or she jumps from command to dismissive comment. On the other hand, *Making Money* (p.96) starts each stanza with one of the senses, creating in five stanzas a sensuous world experienced entirely through money.

The World 'Before we Looked at it'

In studying the poems, you have had to face a number of challenges: to look at each poem in its own right but also to appreciate how these voices are 'familiar', part of an unfolding discourse over a century of change. The wider considerations come after the poems have been experienced, not before. The ideas explored in the Approaches are here to sharpen your own experiences. In this last section therefore, we return to how we may share something of the poets' delight in individual moments of truth or beauty, and in particular to their expression of an 'outer' world.

Activity

Read the first stanza of Jennings' *Beyond Possession* (p.64) and try to understand what she means by *the rose returns / To what it was before we looked at it* (1–2); then try to find one poem from each poet which has made you look at something – perhaps an object in Nature – in an unexpected or fresh way.

Discussion

The six poets react to nature in very different ways. In *'High waving heather 'neath stormy blasts bending'* (p.3) Brontë presents a joyful, dynamic universe *Earth rising to heaven and heaven descending* (4), the tall heather swept in one direction like those twisted pine trees that slant with the wind in *Wuthering Heights*. She speaks of general things yet it is a precise northern landscape. In *To the Blue Bell* (p.5), she focuses on something *wan and frail* (7) which rejoices in its own brief existence *'Glad I bloom and calm I fade'* (15). You might like to consider why this joyful more impersonal mood seems to depart from Brontë's later poetry.

Economy of expression marks Dickinson's distinctive approach. In *'South Winds jostle them'* (p.23), a poem of only 24 words, she conjures by odd inversions and associations a world of flowers and insects which is *What it was before we looked at it* (*Beyond Possession*, p.64 [2]). So in *'A Bird came down the Walk'* (p.26), something awkward becomes a thing of supernatural beauty. And in *'I heard a Fly buzz – when I died'* (p.29) a comical little fly *With Blue-uncertain stumbling Buzz* (13) intervenes at the pious moment when the soul is contemplating immortal perspectives. The poet defines a moment when a self-contained, separate life stumbles into hers.

Plath sometimes finds it difficult to detach herself from objects of perception yet when she does the result is stunning. Only she, it seems, could have described a new-born baby as *a fat gold watch* (*Morning Song*, p.44 [1]) or mushrooms that feed on *crumbs of shadow* (20) and whose *Soft fists* (10) hammer through the soil (*Mushrooms*, p.43), or the cold Atlantic *mouthing ice-cakes* (*A Winter Ship*, p.39 [21]).

Like Brontë, Jennings is drawn to elemental forces – wind, light and water, losing herself in their beauty, so water is *keeping fast in a thousand flowering sprays* (*Fountain*, p.69 [24]) and light is focused in the diamond or explodes in stars or fireworks. In *Anna Liffey* (p.122), Boland, however, fuses her own nature *going home* (178) with the river but also defines its vivid history:

The Viking blades beside it,
The muskets of the Redcoats,
The flames of the Four Courts   (69–71)

and Duffy blends sight and sound together in *The Grammar of Light* (p.100) – the *stars ... stuttering* (20), the way candlelight *slurs* (22) – into a mystical language.

The world is not always seen as beautiful or consoling, often it seems brutal, futile, revolting – compare Duffy's *A Healthy Meal* (p.87) with Plath's *Two Views of a Cadaver Room* (p.40). *Psychopath* (p.92) seems like a horror movie and *The Interrogator* (p.73) opens the door of madness and despair. It would be difficult to describe these poems as 'feminine' in the stereotyped sense of the feminine being something 'tender', 'delicate' or 'restrained'. Each of these poets tries to confront life directly, sometimes achieving even a passionless objectivity.

One criticism of women's writing has been that it is too personal, that women have trouble distancing themselves and over-use the verbs of perception 'I feel ... I hope ... I think'. Virginia Woolf claimed this was not a fault but a strength:

The male atmosphere is disconcerting to me ... what
an abrupt precipice cleaves asunder the male intelligence,
and how they pride themselves upon a point of view.
                        (*The Diary of Virginia Woolf*, ed. A. O. Bell, p.265)

How far do you agree with her? Finally, it is for you to decide on the basis of these poems whether you think the writers are women first or poets first.

Further Reading

Emily Brontë

The Complete Poems of Emily Brontë, (ed.), Janet Gezari (Penguin, 1992).

The Poems of Emily Brontë, (ed.), Derek Roper with Edward Chitham (Clarendon Press, 1995).

Emily Dickinson

The Poems of Emily Dickinson, (ed.), Thomas H. Johnson, 3 volumes (Cambridge, Mass., 1955).

The Complete Poems of Emily Dickinson, (ed.), Thomas H. Johnson, (Faber and Faber, 1970).

Sylvia Plath

The Bell Jar, (Faber and Faber, 1963).

Letters Home, (ed.), Aurelia Plath (Harper and Row, 1975).

Johnny Panic and the Bible of Dreams, (Faber and Faber, 1977).

Collected Poems, (ed.), Ted Hughes (Faber and Faber, 1981).

The Journals of Sylvia Plath, (eds.), Ted Hughes and Frances McCullough (The Dial Press, 1982).

Elizabeth Jennings

Collected Poems, (Carcanet, 1967).

Growing Points, (Carcanet, 1975).

Celebrations and Elegies, (Carcanet, 1982).

Selected Poems, (Carcanet, 1985).

The Bloodaxe Book of Contemporary Women Poets, (ed.), Jeni Couzyn, (Bloodaxe Books, 1985).

Familiar Spirits, (Carcanet, 1994).

Carol Ann Duffy

Standing Female Nude, (Anvil Press Poetry, Ltd., 1985).

Selling Manhattan, (Anvil Press Poetry Ltd., 1987).

The Other Country, (Anvil Press Poetry Ltd., 1990).
Mean Time, (Anvil Press Poetry Ltd., 1993).
Selected Poems, (Penguin, 1994).

Eavan Boland

Selected Poems, (Carcanet, 1989).
Outside History, (Carcanet, 1990).
In a Time of Violence, (Carcanet, 1994).
Object Lessons: The Life of the Woman and the Poet in Our Time, (Carcanet, 1995).
Collected Poems, (Carcanet, 1995).

Critical Works

Miriam Allot (ed.), *The Brontës: The Critical Heritage* (Routledge and Kegan Paul, 1974).

Juliet Barker, *The Brontës* (Weidenfeld and Nicolson, 1994).

Harold Bloom (ed.), *Sylvia Plath: Modern Critical Views* (Chelsea House Publishers, 1989).

Cristanne Miller, *Emily Dickinson A Poet's Grammar* (Harvard University Press, 1987).

Carol Ohmann, 'Emily Brontë in the Hands of Male Critics' (*College English*, *32*, No 8, May 1971).

David Porter, *Dickinson: The Modern Idiom* (Harvard University Press, 1981).

John Robinson, *Emily Dickinson* (Faber and Faber, 1986).

Richard B. Sewall, *The Life of Emily Dickinson*, 2 volumes (New York 1974, London 1976).

Tom Winnifrith, *The Brontës and their Background* (Macmillan, 1973).

General Reading

Juliet Mitchell, *Women: The Largest Revolution: Essays on Feminism, Literature and Psychoanalysis* (Virago Press, 1984).

Ruth Parkin-Gounelas, *Fictions of the Female Self* (Macmillan, 1991).

Virginia Woolf, *Women and Writing* (The Women's Press, 1979).

Tasks

1 Emily Brontë seems to have lived in a purer spiritual atmosphere. Contrast her poetry with that of any one twentieth-century poet whose spiritual struggle seems to you to have been more human.

2 Emily Dickinson's poetry has been described by Paula Bennett as *the violence of withheld emotion* (*Emily Dickinson: Woman Poet*). Discuss the tension between violence and restraint in any three poems in the selection, choosing at least one poem from each century.

3 *Writing is so lonely ... I don't regret being a spinster. Had I married and settled down, I wouldn't have been able to do the writing.* (Elizabeth Jennings, Interview by Rosalyn Chissick, *The Times*, Feb. 1996.) How far do these poems suggest that loneliness, sometimes self-imposed, has been an essential part of the creative process?

4 Eavan Boland writes that at times she thought of herself as an *indoor nature poet* and that her vocabulary was *the kettle and the steam, and the machine in the corner and the kitchen and the baby's bottle*. (Judy Allen-Randolph, 'An Interview with Eavan Boland', *P.N. Review*, volume 20, No 1.) Consider the domestic imagery in any two poets in the selection and the degree to which you find this a limiting or challenging feature of their writing.

5 Many of the poems in the selection are pessimistic in tone. Choose three or four poems which show wit, humour or delight and analyse how this is achieved.

6 Compare the work of one of the nineteenth-century poets in the selection with a poet from the Twentieth century. What features do their writings share and how do they differ?

7 Is anything lost, is anything gained by excluding male poets from this selection?

8 What have you learned from reading these poems about the experience of being a woman? Do you find yourself accepting or questioning the views expressed by any one of the poets?

9 What evidence do you find in this collection of the dominance of a father figure in women's lives?

10 Discuss the use of flashback or memory in this collection.

11 Write about three poems which have given you a distinct sense of place.
12 Compare and contrast two poets in their observation of Nature.
13 Examine the subject of family relationships revealed in this poetry. Select particular images to support your observations.
14 What have you learned about childhood in this collection?
15 What impressions of nineteenth- or twentieth-century society emerge from the collection? Select particular images which illustrate your view.
16 Which poems might successfully be staged in a live performance? Create a script for a radio or studio performance.

Index of First Lines